Y0-FAY-118

The Standard BASIC Dictionary for Programming

John P. Steiner

Prentice-Hall, Inc.
Englewood Cliffs, New Jersey

Business & Professional Division

WITHDRAWN

Prentice-Hall International, Inc., *London*
Prentice-Hall of Australia, Pty. Ltd., *Sydney*
Prentice-Hall Canada, Inc., *Toronto*
Prentice-Hall of India Private Ltd., *New Delhi*
Prentice-Hall of Japan, Inc., *Tokyo*
Prentice-Hall of Southeast Asia Pte. Ltd., *Singapore*
Whitehall Books, Ltd., *Wellington, New Zealand*
Editora Prentice-Hall do Brasil Ltda., *Rio de Janeiro*

© 1984 *by*

PRENTICE-HALL, INC.

Englewood Cliffs, N.J.

All rights reserved. No part of this
book may be reproduced in any form or
by any means, without permission in
writing from the publisher.

Editor: George E. Parker

First Printing. . . . . August 1984

Library of Congress Cataloging in Publication Data

Steiner, John P.
The standard BASIC dictionary for programming.

Bibliography: p.
1. BASIC (Computer program language) I. Title.
QA76.73.B3S83 1984 001.64'24 84-11436
ISBN 0-13-841560-9
ISBN 0-13-841552-8 (PBK)

Printed in the United States of America

Dedication

For Lynn, who humored me for many hours with my new-found passion for computers.

Norma E. Hagan Library
Cumberland College
Williamsburg, Ky. 40769
#10778352

Previous Book by Author

Illustrated Guide to Basic Electronics: With Useful Projects and Experiments

BASIC Dictionary Reference Materials

I wish to thank the following companies, who provided me with documentation in the production of this reference source. Their contributions are appreciated.

Microware Systems Corporation, 5835 Grand Ave., Des Moines, IA 50312. *BASIC09 Programming Language Reference Manual*, 1980, 1983.

North Star Computers, Inc., 14440 Catalina St., San Leandro, CA 94577. *GRAPHICS BASIC*, 1982.

Panasonic Company, Division of Matsushita Electric Corporation of America, One Panasonic Way, Secaucus, NJ 07094. *Microsoft BASIC Reference Guide, Microsoft BASIC Tutorial, Panasonic HHC Manual*, Friends Amis, Inc., 1981.

Zenith Data Systems, 1900 N. Austin Ave., Chicago, IL 60639. *Microsoft Z-BASIC (Z-DOS)*, Copyright by Zenith Data Systems.

NOTE

The BASIC documentation of many computer companies was consulted to verify proper syntax for each BASIC command. I have made every effort to verify that all information is correct. This reference work is based upon documentation from many manufacturers and individuals. If you run into problems, check with your own BASIC manual.

In future editions and reprints of *The Standard BASIC Dictionary for Programming,* we would like to include your version of BASIC. If you note any errors or omissions, please bring them to our attention. We would like to make this dictionary as useful as possible to our readers. Thank you.

The Practical Value of This Reference Book

The reasons why people purchase microcomputers are many and varied. Regardless of your reasons, this extraordinarily useful guide will quickly become invaluable to you. Even those who have previously run only prewritten programs recognize the need to understand BASIC programming.

This book will give you fast access to:

- A dictionary of the BASIC language
- A quick-reference syntax guide
- A cross-reference to similar keywords in BASIC (related to all major brands of hardware)
- A wide range of programming tips and techniques
- Program conversion techniques that can easily be adapted to your needs
- Computer graphics display techniques
- Operation and preventive maintenance techniques
- Computer data and text file programming techniques

As we explore these features, you will be shown how each one will assist you in writing or converting programs and in becoming far more skillful with the BASIC language.

You have undoubtedly found your own computer's reference manual to be a helpful tool in writing and understanding

BASIC programs for your computer. It has probably left several things to be desired, however. For example, you have probably noticed BASIC keywords that you did not fully understand, or you may have tried to convert a program from another computer to run on your own. You may need a quick-reference memory jogger to remind you of the exact syntax of a particular command, or you may simply have an understandable desire to increase your knowledge of the computer's ability or of the BASIC language itself. Helping you to achieve these goals is the primary objective of this book.

In the front of the dictionary, you will find a complete description of a typical directory entry and how each of its parts can be used to make your programming an easier task.

The majority of this reference is a dictionary of the BASIC language. BASIC programs contain lines that generally begin with a line number followed by a keyword. If you cannot understand a keyword or how it operates, just look it up as you would a word in a regular dictionary. Each entry in this dictionary includes a functional definition of the keyword. The definition includes the class of BASIC keyword. The four classes are command, function, statement, and operator. An example of the keyword in a program line is included along with a short description of the results of running that line. A cross-reference is included that references each keyword to other keywords that do the same or a similar operation. This portion of the dictionary entry is most useful when you are attempting to modify a program that was written for a computer other than your own. By using this cross-reference, you may find a keyword that performs a similar operation on your machine, or you may find a routine that will perform in the same manner.

The appendices of this book contain much useful information on program conversions, graphics, disk and tape files, and a useful series of computer and peripheral maintenance information.

Appendices 1 and 2 include several tips on writing BASIC programs or converting programs to run on your computer. They will give you a sharp focus on what can easily be done—and on other things that should not even be attempted. Much time can be wasted trying to enter a routine that has no chance of working because of total incompatibility. You will, therefore, be able to determine easily if a routine is going to work before you begin writing it.

One of the most difficult programming tasks is graphics display. Appendix 3 explains typical graphics formats in BASIC. Included here are definitions of graphics terminology. A basic knowledge of how a machine handles graphics will assist you in understanding and rewriting a particular graphics program segment. Included here are useful guidelines on the application of low-resolution and high-resolution graphics. Also included is a discussion of string graphics techniques.

Essential information on the maintenance of microcomputers and peripherals is included in appendix 4. Appendix 5 covers disk and tape files and their operation. Reference to this section will allow you to rewrite file programs into an acceptable format for your machine. Appendices 6 and 7 contain an ASCII conversion chart and a base conversion chart for your use. In addition, appendix 8 is a quick-reference chart of commonly occurring error messages. Appendix 9 covers mathematical functions derived from BASIC commands. Appendix 10 contains a bibliography of books that you might find useful in finding specific programming information.

Computers covered in the dictionary are manufactured by major computer manufacturers in the United States as well as around the world. Virtually every BASIC interpreter has been documented, and this reference will provide you with one source of documentation that will make your programming simpler and faster.

BASIC programming can be a fascinating and productive endeavor. This book will provide invaluable assistance in your programming tasks, whether you are a novice programmer just writing your first program or an experienced hacker modifying a program to operate on your computer. *The Standard BASIC Dictionary for Programming* will be one of the most used reference sources in your BASIC library.

John Steiner

A

ABS

Type of keyword: Function

ANSI

ABS returns the absolute value of a numeric variable or constant. The absolute value of a number is that number without a positive or negative sign. For example, the absolute value of –28.5 is 28.5. Most BASICs also allow math operations inside the parentheses. In the example below, the variable L will contain the absolute value of the argument. If ABS returns an error message, you may have specified a number that is out of range of the BASIC interpreter.

Typical syntax:

```
L = ABS (10)
L = ABS (Y)
L = ABS (X - 8)
```

ACS

Type of keyword: Function

The ACS function calculates and returns the arccosine of the ratio specified. The ACS is in radians, not degrees. The argument can be expressed as a constant or variable, and most interpreters allow math operations within the argument. In the example below, L will be equal to the arccosine of the variable X. If ACS returns an error message, you may have specified a variable that is out of range.

Typical syntax:

```
L = ACS {X}
```

See also ARCCOS.

ADDR

Type of keyword: Function

ADDR returns the memory address of the specified number or string variable. ADDR can be used to locate and modify BASIC variables from machine language routines. In the example below, L will contain the memory address of the first byte of X. If ADDR returns an error, you may have specified a nonexistent variable.

Typical syntax:

```
L = ADDR {X}
```

See also VARPTR.

AND

Type of keyword: Operator

AND is used in conjunction with IF–THEN statements to test for multiple conditions. In the example below, if both A = 15 and B = 15, then X will equal 20; otherwise X will equal 10. Another application is in Boolean algebra. The second example demonstrates the syntax. If X and Y are not equal to zero, they are considered to have values of 1. If they are zero, they are zero. In this example, a 1 will be assigned to B if the values of X and Y are both not equal to zero. If either X or Y is zero, then B will equal zero. Normally, AND will not return an error message.

Typical syntax:

```
IF A = 15 AND B = 15 THEN X = 20 ELSE X = 10
LET B = X AND Y
```

See also LAND.

APPEND filename

Type of keyword: Command, Statement

APPEND is a disk BASIC command that allows a data file to be appended. After a file is opened, the file pointer is set to the end of a file rather than to its beginning. New data written to the file are placed at the back of the file. In the second example, volume, slot, and drive number options are shown. If an error message is returned, you may have specified an incorrect or nonexistent filename or option. Some systems allow BASIC programs to be appended in a similar format.

Typical syntax:

```
APPEND HELLO
APPEND PROGRAM, 1, 6, 2
```

See also MERGE.

ARC

Type of keyword: Statement

ARC is a graphics command that is used to draw a partial ellipse. In the first example below, the arc is drawn with a horizontal radius of 10 and a vertical radius of 12. The ellipse is drawn from an angle of 90 degrees to an angle of 180 degrees. In the second example, the arc is filled with a pattern number. Any numeric expression may be used for the angle parameters. If you receive an error message, you may have specified an out-of-range value for radius or pattern number.

Typical syntax:

```
ARC 10, 12, 90, 180
ARC 5, 10, -10, 10, 100
```

See also CHORDSLICE, CIRCLE, ELLIPSE.

ARCCOS

Type of keyword: Function

ARCCOS will return the arccosine of any number between −1 and +1. The result is in radians rather than degrees. In the first example, the variable X will contain the arccosine of variable L. If ARCCOS returns an error, you may have specified an out-of-range variable or constant.

Typical syntax:

```
X = ARCCOS (L)
PRINT ARCCOS (-.32)
```

See also ACS, COS.

ARCSIN

Type of keyword: Function

The ARCSIN function returns the arcsine of an angle expressed in radians. The argument can be either constant or variable format and can usually be a mathematic operation. In the first example below, X will contain the arcsine of the variable L. If

ARCSIN returns an error, you may have specified an out-of-range argument.

Typical syntax:

```
X = ARCSIN {L}
PRINT ARCSIN {.5}
```

See also ASN, SIN.

ARCTAN

Type of keyword: Function

The ARCTAN function returns the arctangent of an angle measured in radians. The angle can be a constant or a variable and must be converted to radians. In the first example, the variable X will contain the arctangent of the variable L. If ARCTAN returns an error, you may have specified an out-of-range variable or constant.

Typical syntax:

```
X = ARCTAN {L}
PRINT ARCTAN {.5}
```

See also ATN, TAN.

ASC

Type of keyword: Function

ASC returns the ASCII code of the first letter in the specified string. See appendix 6 for a listing of the ASCII code. In the example below, L contains the ASCII value of the string specified. If ASC returns an error message, you may have specified a string that has too many characters or a nonexistent string. Some computers will not allow ASC to be used with strings longer than a single character.

Typical syntax:

```
L = ASC {"B"}
L = ASC {X$}
```

See also CODE.

ASN

Type of keyword: Function

The ASN function calculates and returns the arcsine of the ratio specified. The ASN is an angle measured in radians, not degrees. The argument can be expressed as a constant or a variable, and most interpreters allow math operations within the argument. In the example below, L will be equal to the arcsine of the variable X. If ASN returns an error message, you may have specified a variable that is out of range.

Typical syntax:

```
L = ASN {X}
```

See also ARCSIN.

AT
See PRINT@

ATN

Type of keyword: Function

ANSI

The ATN function calculates and returns the arctangent of the ratio specified. The ATN is an angle measured in radians, not degrees. The argument can be expressed as a constant or a variable, and most interpreters allow math operations within the argument. In the example below, L will be equal to the arctangent of the variable X. If ATN returns an error message, you may have specified a variable that is out of range.

Typical syntax:

```
L = ATN {X}
```

See also ARCTAN.

ATTACH

Type of keyword: Command, Statement

ATTACH is used when you wish to attach a device specified with its device number to the logical unit number. In the example below, the printer (device number 68) is attached to logical unit number 2. The number sign must be included. Devices must be attached before the computer recognizes that they are connected. If you receive an error message, you may have specified an out-of-range device or unit number.

Typical syntax:

```
ATTACH 68 TO #2
```

AUDIO

Type of keyword: Command, Statement

AUDIO is a system-specific command that turns on the sound channel between the cassette player and the TV monitor. It allows sounds recorded on cassette to be heard by the operator. Once it is turned on, audio can be turned off by command. Error messages may also shut off the audio.

Typical syntax:

```
AUDIO ON
AUDIO OFF
```

AUTO

Type of keyword: Command

AUTO allows the computer to generate BASIC line numbers for you. Though exact syntax varies from one machine to another, there are usually arguments that allow you to specify the start number and increment. In the second example, the computer will start numbering at line 100 and increment in steps of 10. There is usually a special key or key sequence to disable the AUTO function once it is in use. On many machines, the BREAK or CONTROL C will work. If the computer generates a line number already in use, an asterisk is often printed next to the number. Just press ENTER if you want the old line to remain. If AUTO returns an error, you may have specified an out-of-range line number or increment.

Typical syntax:

```
AUTO
AUTO 100, 10
```

See also NUMBER.

AXIS

Type of keyword: Statement

AXIS is a graphics command that will draw a grid axis on the display device. The syntax for AXIS, as shown in the first example below, is AXIS xtic, ytic, xzero, yzero. In the example, the grid center is at 10 vertical and 10 horizontal. No tics are drawn, as xtic and ytic are set to zero. The second example demonstrates the same grid with tics drawn at intervals of 5. Variables as well as constants are allowed, as shown in the third example. If AXIS returns an error, you may have specified an out-of-range variable, constant, or coordinate.

Typical syntax:

```
AXIS 0, 0, 0, 0
AXIS 5, 5, 0, 0
AXIS A, B, X + Y, C * D
```

B

BACKUP

Type of keyword: Command

BACKUP is used to create a copy of a disk for archival purposes. In the example below, the disk in drive zero will be copied to the disk in drive 1. Many systems allow single drive backup by leaving out or duplicating the source drive number. You will be prompted to switch disks, as the data are loaded into memory and readied to be transferred to the destination disk. If BACKUP returns an error message, you may have specified an improper drive number.

Typical syntax:

```
BACKUP 0 TO 1
BACKUP 0 TO 0
BACKUP 0
```

See also COPY.

BASE

Type of keyword: Command, Statement

ANSI

BASE is used to set the minimum number allowed in an array to zero or 1. In the first example, the minimum value of the array is zero. Executing the second example will give the array L a minimum value of 1. Choosing the base will define that base for all arrays that are dimensioned in the program. If you receive an error message, you may have dimensioned an array before stating the base, or you may have used a number other than zero or 1.

Typical syntax:

```
BASE 0
BASE 1
```

See also OPTION BASE.

BEEP

Type of keyword: Command, Statement

BEEP sounds a tone in the speaker. It can be used in any application where some kind of audio warning or notice is required. In the example below, BEEP will sound a tone. Normally, BEEP will not generate an error statement.

Typical syntax:

```
BEEP
```

See also CALL SOUND, PLAY, SOUND.

BLOAD filename

Type of keyword: Command

BLOAD is a disk BASIC command used to load a binary file from the disk. If no start address is specified, the start address stored using BSAVE will be used. If an address is specified, as in the second example, the program will be loaded there. In the third example, slot, drive number, and volume options are shown. If an error message is returned, you may have specified an incorrect or nonexistent filename or option.

Typical syntax:

```
BLOAD PROGRAM
BLOAD FILE, A4096
BLOAD PICTURE, A2000, 1, 6, 2
```

See also BRUN, CLOAD, CLOADM, LOADM.

BREAK

Type of keyword: Command, Statement

BREAK is used to stop a program in the middle of its execution. It is often used to assist in debugging and testing program flow. If used in a program as in the first example, BREAK will stop program execution at that line. In the second example, the program will stop when line 1000 is executed. This command may be entered in immediate or program mode. In the third example, the BREAK command will stop program operation at line 1000 and again at line 1050. To resume program execution, enter CONTINUE. Some systems use CO, CON, or CONT. To remove a breakpoint, enter UNBREAK in some cases; in others, just delete the line containing the BREAK. If BREAK returns an error, you may have specified a nonexistent or out-of-range line number.

Typical syntax:

```
10 BREAK
BREAK 1000
BREAK 1000, 1050
10 BREAK 10, 50, 90
```

See also CONT, CONTINUE, PAUSE, STOP, UNBREAK.

BRUN filename

Type of keyword: Command, Statement

BRUN is a disk BASIC command used to load and execute a machine language file from the disk. If no start address is specified, the start address stored using BSAVE will be used. If an address is specified, as in the second example, the program will be loaded there. Machine language programs must be relocatable if they are loaded using the A option. In the third example, slot, drive number, and volume options are shown. If an error message is returned, you may have specified an incorrect or nonexistent filename or option.

Typical syntax:

```
BRUN PROGRAM
BRUN FILE, A4096
BRUN PICTURE, A2000, 1, 6, 2
```

See also CLOAD, CLOADM, LOADM, RUN.

BSAVE filename

Type of keyword: Command

BSAVE is a disk BASIC command used to save a binary file on the disk. Two arguments are required: start address of the data and data length. In the second example, slot, drive number, and volume options are shown. If an error message is returned, you may have specified an incorrect or nonexistent filename or option.

Typical syntax:

```
BSAVE PROGRAM, A1000, L100
BSAVE PICTURE, A2000, L50, 1, 6, 2
```

See also CSAVE, CSAVEM, SAVEM.

BYE

Type of keyword: Command

BYE is used when you wish to exit the BASIC interpreter and return to the main menu or disk operating system. At that point you may choose a program to edit or run. In many systems BYE will return control to the disk operating system. Normally, BYE will not return an error message.

Typical syntax:

```
BYE
```

See also SYSTEM.

C

CALL

Type of keyword: Command, Statement

CALL is used to transfer control from a BASIC program to a machine language routine. The argument is the memory location, usually in decimal, where the machine language routine begins. The machine language routine will be executed, and when it is done a return from subroutine (RTS) opcode in machine language will usually return control to BASIC. In some systems, BASIC variables may be passed to the routine in an argument list following the command, as in the second example. If CALL returns an error, you may have specified a number that is out of range.

Typical syntax:

```
CALL 32749
CALL 4000 (X, Y$, Z)
```

See also DEF USR, SYS, USR.

CALL CHAR

Type of keyword: Statement

CALL CHAR is used to redefine a character to be displayed on the screen. Characters are organized on an 8 × 8 grid, and a binary notation determines which portion of the grid is to be set or reset. In the example below, X$ contains the shape of the new character, and the number 37 is the ASCII value for the percent sign. We are redefining the percent key as a solid block. Either the ASCII value or the string can be defined as a variable or a constant, as in the second example. If CALL CHAR returns an error message, you may have specified an out-of-range variable or incorrect string format.

Typical syntax:

```
X$ = "FFFFFFFFFFFFFFFF"
CALL CHAR (37, X$)
CALL CHAR (N, "FFFFFFFFFFFFFFFF")
```

CALL CLEAR

Type of keyword: Statement

CALL CLEAR clears the video screen of information and returns the cursor to the upper left corner. In the example below, after execution the monitor screen will be cleared. Normally, CALL CLEAR will not return an error message.

Typical syntax:

```
CALL CLEAR
```

See also CALL CLEAR, CLEAR, CLS, HOME.

CALL COLOR

Type of keyword: Statement

CALL COLOR is used to determine which character set is being used and the foreground and background colors. In the example below, character set 3 is being used on foreground color 1 and background color 2. The numbers can be specified as either variable or constant, as demonstrated in the second example. If CALL COLOR returns an error message, you may have specified an out-of-range or incorrect variable.

Typical syntax:

```
CALL COLOR (3, 1, 2)
CALL COLOR (X, Y, Z)
```

See also COLOR, SETCOLOR.

CALL GCHAR

Type of keyword: Statement

CALL GCHAR is used to allow a program to identify a character that is being displayed on the screen. In the example below, the ASCII value of the character located at row 10, column 5, will be stored in variable L. Row and column may be specified as either constants or variables; L is a numeric variable. If CALL GCHAR returns an error, you may have specified an out-of-range screen coordinate or improper variable.

Typical syntax:

```
CALL GCHAR (10, 5, L)
```

See also POINT.

CALL HCHAR

Type of keyword: Statement

CALL HCHAR is used to specify and print a character at a given point on the screen. In the example below, the exclamation point will be printed at screen location (10, 10). The location, quantity, and character value can be specified as either a constant or a variable. In the second example, ten characters will be printed in a horizontal row. If CALL HCHAR returns an error, you may have specified a number that is out of range or an incorrect variable.

Typical syntax:

```
CALL HCHAR (10, 10, 33)
CALL HCHAR (10, 10, 33, 10)
```

See also CALL VCHAR, CSRLIN, HTAB, LOCATE, POSITION, PRINT @, VTAB.

CALL JOYST

Type of keyword: Statement

CALL JOYST is used when you wish to evaluate the position of the joystick controllers. The first number specifies which controller is desired. The second and third numbers must be variables, which will represent the position of the joystick. In the first example, controller number 1 is being evaluated. H and V will contain either a +4, zero, or −4, depending upon joystick position. A zero indicates center, +4 represents up or right, −4 represents left or down. If CALL JOYST returns an error, you may have specified an incorrect or out-of-range number or variable.

Typical syntax:

```
CALL JOYST (1, H, V)
CALL JOYST (X, A, B)
```

See also JOYSTK, PADDLE, PDL, STICK.

CALL KEY

Type of keyword: Statement

CALL KEY scans the keyboard looking for a keypress. If one is found, the specified variable will hold the ASCII value of the key pressed. CALL KEY allows keyboard input without stopping program execution to wait for an ENTER or RETURN key. There are three numeric values associated with the CALL KEY statement. In the example below, the ASCII value of the key being pressed is stored in variable X. Variable Z contains a status indicator. This variable will contain one of three numbers after executing CALL KEY. If a new key is being pressed, Z will contain a 1. If the key being pressed is the same key as last press, Z will contain a −1. If no key is being pressed, Z will contain a zero. If CALL KEY returns an error, you may have specified an incorrect variable.

Typical syntax:

```
CALL KEY (0, X, Z)
```

See also GET str, INCHAR$, INKEY$.

CALL SCREEN

Type of keyword: Statement

CALL SCREEN is used to clear the screen to a different background color. A background screen can be any of 16 colors. In the example below, the screen color is being set to color number 5. The number can be either a constant or a variable. If CALL SCREEN returns an error, you may have specified an out-of-range or incorrect variable.

Typical syntax:

```
CALL SCREEN (5)
CALL SCREEN (X)
```

See also CLS, HOME.

CALL SOUND

Type of keyword: Statement

CALL SOUND is used to generate sound output from the monitor audio system. The argument contains three numbers: duration in milliseconds, frequency in hertz, and volume. In the first example, a 1000-hertz tone lasting 100 milliseconds at low volume would be heard. Frequency range is from 110 hertz to 44,000 hertz. Duration is from 1 to 4275 milliseconds, and volume range is from zero to 30, with zero being the loudest tone. The numbers can be expressed as either a constant or a variable. If CALL SOUND returns an error, you may have specified an out-of-range or incorrect variable.

Typical syntax:

```
CALL SOUND (100, 1000, 29)
```

See also BEEP, PLAY, SOUND.

CALL VCHAR

Type of keyword: Statement

CALL VCHAR is used to specify and print a character at a given point on the screen. In the example below, the exclamation point will be printed at screen location (10, 10). The location, quantity, and character number can be specified as either a constant or a variable. In the second example, ten characters will be printed in a vertical row. If CALL VCHAR returns an error, you may have specified a number that is out of range or an incorrect variable.

Typical syntax:

```
CALL VCHAR (10, 10, 33)
CALL VCHAR (10, 10, 33, 10)
```

See also CALL HCHAR, CSRLIN, HTAB, LOCATE, POSITION, PRINT @, VTAB.

CAT

See CATALOG.

CATALOG

Type of keyword: Command, Statement

COMMAND accesses and displays a disk directory. An optional drive number is allowed, which will specify which drive to use. Normally, CATALOG will not return an error message unless you specify an incorrect drive number. CAT is often accepted on many systems.

Typical syntax:

```
CATALOG
CATALOG, D1
CAT 1
CAT #1
```

See also DIR, FILES.

CDBL

Type of keyword: Function

CDBL is used to convert a number from single to double precision. While double-precision numbers take up more memory in the computer, they are more accurate. In many computers, single-precision numbers are often carried out to the eighth decimal place, as in .99999999, while double precision allows numbers to be calculated to 16 places for higher accuracy. In the example below, the variable Y will be printed as a 16-place number. Normally, CDBL will not return an error message.

Typical syntax:

```
Y = 5/8
PRINT CDBL {Y}
```

See also DEF DBL, DEF INT, DEF SNG, DEF STR.

CHAIN

Type of keyword: Statement

CHAIN is a disk BASIC command used from within a BASIC program. CHAIN loads and runs the program specified in the filename but does not reset or destroy any variables. This allows data created by one program to be accessed from another. In the second example, volume, slot, and drive number options are shown. If an error message is returned, you may have specified an incorrect or nonexistent filename or option. Some machines use arguments that specify which, if any, variables will be chained. Some do not allow the retention of previously defined variables or may require quotation marks around the filename.

Typical syntax:

```
CHAIN HELLO
CHAIN PROGRAM, 1, 6, 2
```

See also PARAM.

CHORDSLICE

Type of keyword: Statement

CHORDSLICE is a command used to draw a partial circle and put a baseline that creates a segment of a circle. Horizontal and vertical radii are specified in the first arguments, followed by starting and ending angles. In the first example, an ellipse is drawn that has a horizontal radius of 5 and a vertical radius of 10. The beginning and ending angles are also specified, in this case zero and 90 degrees. Variables and constants may be specified.

Typical syntax:

```
CHORDSLICE 5, 5, 0, 90
CHORDSLICE X, Y, A, B
```

See also ARC, CIRCLE, ELLIPSE.

CHR$

Type of keyword: Function

CHR$ converts a number to its ASCII character. For example, PRINT CHR$ (65) prints the letter A on the screen or printer. See appendix 6 for an ASCII code conversion chart. If CHR$ returns an error, you have probably specified an out-of-range number. The ASCII code range is from zero to 127, though many computers have an extended range of zero to 255.

Typical syntax:

```
L$ = CHR$ (66)
D$ = CHR$ (13) + CHR$ (4)
```

CINT

Type of keyword: Function

CINT is used to convert a number from single or double precision to an integer by rounding the fractional portion of the number. In the example below, the computer will print the number 100. If CINT returns an error, you may have specified a number that is out of range.

Typical syntax:

```
PRINT CINT (99.59)
```

See also CDBL, CSNG, FIX, INT.

CIRCLE

Type of keyword: Command, Statement

CIRCLE is a graphics command that draws a circle at the specified coordinates. Several options may be available. In the example below, a circle will be drawn with its center at XY coordinate (100, 100). It will be a radius of 10 pixels, with a color of 2. In the second example, a height/width ratio is specified, making an ellipse. Also specified are start and end points, which make the circle into an arc. If CIRCLE returns an error message, you may have specified illegal coordinates, out-of-range radius, or improper color number. Numbers that appear after the radius will vary depending upon the system; check your documentation.

Typical syntax:

```
CIRCLE (100, 100), 10, 2
CIRCLE (40, 40), 14, 3, .4, .5, .75
```

See also ARC, CHORDSLICE, ELLIPSE, PIESLICE.

CLEAR

Type of keyword: Command, Statement

CLEAR resets all numeric variables to zero and all string variables to null. On some computers, CLEAR will remove a resident program from memory. Normally, CLEAR will not return an error message. On the North Star series of computers, CLEAR will clear the graphics screen.

Typical syntax:

```
CLEAR
```

See also CALL CLEAR, CLEAR number, CLR, CLS, ERASE, HOME.

CLEAR number

Type of keyword: Command, Statement

CLEAR with an argument reserves string space in a computer's memory. The argument can usually be either a constant or a variable. In many machines, CLEAR without a variable (*see* CLEAR) will automatically reserve a default value for strings. In addition, it will reset all variables to zero or null. In the example below, 500 bytes of string space are reserved. If CLEAR returns an error message, you have probably specified a number less than zero or greater than the memory requirements of the system. Some systems have a double argument, such as CLEAR 200, 16000. In this context, 200 bytes are reserved for strings, and the highest memory location that can be used by BASIC is 16000.

Typical syntax:

```
CLEAR 500
```

See also CLEAR, CLR, HIMEM, MEMSET.

CLOAD

Type of keyword: Command, Statement

CLOAD is a system-specific command used to load a program from cassette into the computer. When used as above, the next program on tape will be accepted. Some systems have various options. CLOAD "filename" will search the tape and load the program named "filename". CLOAD? "filename" will compare the tape program to the program in memory and return an error message if the two differ. On some computers, CLOAD* (array) can be used to load an array previously stored on tape.

Typical syntax:

```
CLOAD
CLOAD "HELLO"
```

See also BLOAD, CLOADM, LOAD, LOADM, RECALL.

CLOADM

Type of keyword: Command, Statement

CLOADM loads a machine language program into memory. CLOADM "filename" searches tape and loads the program called "filename". CLOADM "filename" offset loads a program called "filename" and offsets its specified load start address by the number specified. In the example below, the program "MONITOR" is loaded 1000 bytes above the normal loading address. If an error message is returned, you have possibly specified a filename that is of incorrect format or an impossible offset.

Typical syntax:

```
CLOADM
CLOADM "MONITOR"
CLOADM "MONITOR", 1000
```

See also BLOAD, CLOAD, LOAD, LOADM.

CLOSE

Type of keyword: Command, Statement

CLOSE is used in disk and tape files to purge the file buffer and write end-of-file information to the media. As with all disk commands, there are variations. Some systems will ask you to specify the buffer number to close, while others specify the filename. In the first example, disk buffer number 1 will be closed, and end-of-file and catalog information will be written to the disk. The buffer number can be a constant or a variable. In the second example, the file, FILENAME, will be closed. Most computers accept CLOSE with no buffer or file specified. When used in this manner, CLOSE will close all open files. Some systems omit the number sign; others require it. If CLOSE returns an error message, you may have specified an incorrect filename or a buffer number out of range. See appendix 5 for more information.

Typical syntax:

```
CLOSE #1
CLOSE FILENAME
```

See also OPEN, READ, WRITE.

CLR

Type of keyword: Command, Statement

CLR clears the video screen of information and returns the cursor to the upper left corner. On some systems, CLR will reset all variables to zero and all strings to null. Normally, no error message will be returned.

Typical syntax:

```
CLR
```

See also CALL CLEAR, CLEAR, CLS, HOME.

CLS

Type of keyword: Command, Statement

CLS clears the video screen of information and returns the cursor to the upper left corner. Color computers may have a variation, as follows: CLS n clears the screen to the specified color number. Normally, no error message will be returned.

Typical syntax:

```
CLS
CLS 5
```

See also CALL CLEAR, CALL SCREEN, CLEAR, CLR, HOME.

CMD

Type of keyword: Statement

CMD is used to transfer output from the screen to another device, such as a disk drive or printer. The device to be printed to must be opened first; then a CMD command to the opened buffer must be given. In the example below, the CMD will route all PRINTs to buffer number 1. To restore screen printing, just close the open buffer. You could use this command to LIST a program on the printer or into a disk file for editing. If CMD returns an error, you may have specified an incorrect or out-of-range buffer number.

Typical syntax:

```
CMD 1
```

See also LLIST, PRINT #.

CO

See CONTINUE.

CODE

Type of keyword: Command, Statement

CODE returns the ASCII code of a single letter string. In the example below, L contains the ASCII value of X$. On the Timex/Sinclair series of computers, CODE returns a different value from the ASCII value, as Sinclair does not use the ASCII code. If CODE returns an error message, you may have specified a string that has too many characters or a nonexistent string.

Typical syntax:

```
CODE
```

See also ASC.

COLOR

Type of keyword: Command, Statement

COLOR is used to specify a specific color on several color-oriented computers. On some computers, a single color number indicates the foreground color or color that will be used next. The color number can usually be either a constant or a variable, and math operations are usually allowed. With others, a foreground and background color can be specified. If COLOR returns an error, you may have specified an out-of-range value or unavailable device.

Typical syntax:

```
COLOR = 3
COLOR 2, 4
```

See also CALL COLOR, SETCOLOR.

COM

Type of keyword: Command, Statement

COM is used to change various parameters regarding the communications adapter. COM has several options. In the first example, the communications port number 1 is enabled, allowing access by BASIC to data on the specified COM line. The second example disables the COM action. ON COM GOSUB will cause a branch to occur when data enter the communications port. If COM returns an error, you may have specified an out-of-range buffer number or inappropriate option.

Typical syntax:

```
COM (1) ON
COM (1) OFF
ON COM (1) GOSUB 1000
```

COMMON

Type of keyword: Statement

COMMON is used in conjunction with CHAIN and tells the computer which variables are to be passed to the program being chained. If COMMON returns an error, you may not have properly dimensioned any array(s) specified.

Typical syntax:

```
COMMON X, Y, Z$, A()
```

See also CHAIN.

CON
See CONTINUE.

CONT

Type of keyword: Command

Used in immediate mode, CONT will resume program execution after using the STOP statement. Enter CONT to resume a program after using the BREAK key or CONTROL C. Program variables are not reset, and program execution continues from where it stopped. An error message will be returned if a program has not been stopped or after an EDIT command.

Typical syntax:

```
CONT
```

See also BREAK, CONTINUE, PAUSE, STOP.

CONTINUE

Type of keyword: Command

Used in immediate mode, CONTINUE will resume program execution after using the BREAK statement or BREAK key. Program variables are not reset, and program execution continues from where it stopped. Optionally, entering CONT, CON, or CO is allowed, depending upon the machine. An error message will be returned if a program has not been stopped or after editing the program.

Typical syntax:

```
CONTINUE
CONT
CON
CO
```

See also BREAK, CONT, PAUSE, STOP.

COPY

Type of keyword: Command, Statement

COPY is used to copy disk files to another disk. In some machines, COPY will copy an entire disk. One or two drives may be used in most cases. If COPY returns an error message, you may have specified an improper filename or drive number. On the Timex/Sinclair and Epson series of computers, COPY is used to send a copy of the screen contents to the printer. The word COPY is all that is required to do a screen dump, as demonstrated in the third example.

Typical syntax:

```
COPY "FILENAME/EXT"
COPY "FILENAME/EXT:0" TO "FILENAME/EXT:1"
COPY
```

See also BACKUP.

COS

Type of keyword: Function

ANSI

The COS function returns the cosine of an angle given in radians. In the example below, L will equal the cosine of variable X. If COS returns an error, you may have specified an out-of-range or illegal variable.

Typical syntax:

```
L = COS(X)
```

See also ACS, ARCCOS.

CREATE

Type of keyword: Statement

CREATE will initiate a new file of the specified filename. The file will be entered into the disk directory and space reserved in accordance with DOS standards. In the second example, two options to CREATE are demonstrated. A file designated "filespec" will be created that contains 10 256-byte sectors. The filetype will contain a number representing an allowable file type. In this example, 3 indicates a BASIC data file. BASIC 09 has access mode options of WRITE, UPDATE, or EXEC. If CREATE returns an error, you may have used an improper filename, used a full or write-protected diskette, or specified an option that is out of range.

Typical syntax:

```
CREATE FILESPEC
CREATE TESTFILE, 10, 3
```

See also OPEN.

CSAVE

Type of keyword: Command

CSAVE creates a tape program file that can be accessed by using the CLOAD command. On some machines, a filename can be assigned using CSAVE "filename". The variation CSAVE "filename", A will save a program on tape using the ASCII format on some machines. In ASCII format, BASIC keywords are not tokenized, allowing programs to be loaded into text editors and other utilities for modification, editing, and so on. Tokenizing converts the keyword into a compact form for more efficient memory storage. CSAVE* on some systems allows the saving of an array to tape. An error message usually indicates that an improper filename has been specified.

Typical syntax:

```
CSAVE
CSAVE "HELLO"
CSAVE "HELLO", A
```

See also SAVE, STORE.

CSAVEM

Type of keyword: Command, Statement

CSAVEM creates a tape machine-language file that can be accessed by using the CLOADM command. An eight-letter filename is specified, as are the start, end, and execute addresses. In the example below, the program "filename" is being saved. Start address is at memory location 16100, end address is at 16384, and program execution will begin at 16120. If an error message is returned, you may have specified an improper filename or nonexistent or out-of-range memory locations.

Typical syntax:

```
CSAVEM "FILENAME", 16000, 16384, 16100
```

See also CSAVE, SAVE.

CSNG

Type of keyword: Function

CSNG is used to convert a number from double to single precision. While double-precision numbers take up more memory in the computer, they are more accurate. In many computers, single-precision numbers are often carried out to the eighth decimal place, as in .99999999, while double precision allows numbers to be calculated to 16 places for higher accuracy. In the example below, the variable Y will be printed as a single-precision number. Normally, CSNG will not return an error message.

Typical syntax:

```
Y = 5/8
PRINT CSNG {Y}
```

See also CDBL, CINT, DEF DBL, DEF INT, DEF SNG.

CSRLIN

Type of keyword: Function

The CSRLIN function is used to determine the current cursor line position. In the example below, the variable Y will contain the number of the line that the cursor is on. CSRLIN can be used in conjunction with POS to determine the exact cursor location. Normally, CSRLIN will not return an error.

Typical syntax:

```
Y = CSRLIN
```

See also CALL HCHAR, CALL VCHAR, HTAB, LOCATE, POS, POSITION, VTAB.

CVD

Type of keyword: Function

CVD converts a coded string variable back to the double-precision number it represents. CVD is used in conjunction with MKD$ to code numbers to a constant-length string. The string can then be placed in a random access disk file, keeping the field organization and length intact. If CVD returns an error message, you may have specified a nonexistent string or a string that was not coded with MKD$.

Typical syntax:

```
PRINT CVD {AF$}
L = CVD {AF$}
```

See also CVI, CVN, CVS, MKD$, MKI$, MKN$, MKS$.

CVI

Type of keyword: Function

CVI converts a coded string variable back to the number it represents. CVI is used in conjunction with the MKI$ to code numbers to a constant-length string. The string can then be placed in a random access disk file, keeping the field organization and length intact. If CVI returns an error message, you may have specified a nonexistent string or a string that was not coded with MKI$.

Typical syntax:

```
PRINT CVI {AF$}
L = CVI {AF$}
```

See also CVD, CVN, CVS, MKD$, MKI$, MKN$, MKS$.

CVN

Type of keyword: Function

CVN converts a coded string variable back to the number it represents. CVN is used in conjunction with MKN$ to code all numbers to a constant-length string. The string can then be placed in a random access disk file, keeping the field organization intact. If CVN returns an error message, you may have specified a nonexistent string or a string that was not coded with MKN$.

Typical syntax:

```
PRINT CVN {AF$}
L = CVN {AF$}
```

See also CVD, CVI, CVS, MKD$, MKI$, MKN$, MKS$.

CVS

Type of keyword: Function

CVS converts a coded string variable back to the single-precision number it represents. CVS is used in conjunction with MKS$ to code numbers to a constant-length string. The string can then be placed in a random access disk file, keeping the field organization and length intact. If CVS returns an error message, you may have specified a nonexistent string or a string that was not coded with MKS$.

Typical syntax:

```
PRINT CVS {AF$}
L = CVS {AF$}
```

See also CVD, CVI, CVN, MKD$, MKI$, MKN$, MKS$.

D

DATA

Type of keyword: Statement

ANSI

DATA is used to precede lines of program operating data. Program data always remain the same unless DATA lines are edited. Both string and numeric data are supported, and items are usually separated with a comma. Some systems require quotes around string data; others only require the quotes if the data include spaces or commas. Some systems accept D. as abbreviation for DATA. DATA usually only returns an error if you try to assign string data to a numeric variable. See the READ statement for more information.

Typical syntax:

```
DATA 10, 20, 30
DATA 10, HELLO, "JONES, JOHN"
```

See also READ.

DATE$

Type of keyword: Command, Statement

DATE$ is a variable that sets or returns the current date. In the first and second examples, the current date is being assigned to DATE$. In the third example, the current DATE will be printed. If DATE$ returns an error, you may have specified an out-of-range or incorrect variable type.

Typical syntax:

```
DATE$ = 01-01-83
DATE$ = 01-01-83
PRINT DATE$
```

DAY

Type of keyword: Command, Statement

DAY is a numeric variable used in Epson computers to allow the computer to record the number of the day of the week in memory. The first example shows the correct syntax to assign the day number, while the second example allows the day of the week to be printed. Sunday is the first day of the week in the system. If DAY returns an error, you may have specified an out-of-range or incorrect variable type.

Typical syntax:

```
DAY = 7
IF DAY = 7 THEN PRINT "SATURDAY"
```

DEF

Type of keyword: Statement

The define command (DEF) is a powerful mathematical feature. Using DEF allows you to create your own BASIC functions. The syntax is DEF name (variable list) = formula. You assign a name to the function and a variable. The formula is the function you want performed when the function is called. In the first example, function L is the name, and variable P equals P divided by 2. The second line calls the function in the first example. If an error message is returned, you may have incorrectly defined the function or failed to define the function named.

Typical syntax:

```
DEF L = P/2
PRINT SIN (L)
```

See also DEF FN.

DEF DBL

Type of keyword: Statement

Define double (DEF DBL) allows you to define a variable as a double-precision type. Computers that allow definition of variable types usually allow the declaration of integer, single or double precision, and string variable types. On most systems, failure to define a variable usually defaults it to single precision. Double precision allows greater accuracy, while integer variables use the least amount of memory. Once variables are declared, normally all variables beginning with the specified letter will be of the type defined. If you receive an error message, you may have specified an incorrect variable type, as in DEF DBL A$.

Typical syntax:

```
DEF DBL X
DEF DBL A, B, C
```

See also DEF INT, DEF SNG, DEF STR.

DEFFIL

Type of keyword: Command, Statement

DEFFIL is used to define and store a program or data file in memory. The syntax is shown in the first example, where a file is stored in memory that has a record size of 20. The second example demonstrates the offset option, which gives the number of bytes from the beginning of the file where record zero will be placed. To use the memory file, the syntax for GET and PUT in disk random BASIC is similar. Data stored in the memory file are not lost when the computer is shut off, nor by the RUN or CLEAR commands. If DEFFIL returns an error, you may have specified an incorrect offset or out-of-range record size.

Typical syntax:

```
DEFFIL 20
DEFFIL 10, 10
```

See also GET, PUT.

DEF FN

Type of keyword: Statement

ANSI

The define function (DEF FN) command is a powerful mathematical feature. DEF FN allows you to create your own BASIC functions. The syntax is DEF FN name (variable list) = formula. You assign a name to the function and a variable. The formula is the function you want performed when the function is called. In the first example, function A is the name, and variable X equals X divided by 2. The second example calls the function that is defined in the first example. If an error message is returned, you may have incorrectly defined the function or failed to define the function named.

Typical syntax:

```
DEF FNA (X) = X/2
L = FNA (Y)
```

See also DEF.

DEF INT

Type of keyword: Statement

The define integer (DEF INT) allows you to define a variable as an integer type. Computers that allow definition of variable types usually allow the declaration of integer, single or double precision, and string variable types. On most systems, failure to define a variable usually defaults it to single precision. Double precision allows greater accuracy, while integer variables use the least amount of memory. Once variables are declared, normally all variables beginning with the specified letter will be of the type defined. If you receive an error message, you may have specified an incorrect variable type, as in DEF INT A$.

Typical syntax:

```
DEF INT X
DEF INT A, B, C
```

See also DEF DBL, DEF SNG, DEF STR.

DEF SEG

Type of keyword: Command, Statement

DEF SEG assigns a new address to be used by a machine language function call. Computers use DEF SEG in conjunction with the BLOAD, BSAVE, PEEK, POKE, CALL, or user-defined function calls. The address specified must be within the memory map. Machine language calls following the DEF SEG statement will refer to the address defined unless otherwise specified. In the example below, the memory segment is defined at location 16384. If DEF SEG returns an error, you may have specified an out-of-range address.

Typical syntax:

```
DEF SEG = 16384
```

See also BLOAD, BSAVE, CALL, DEF USR, PEEK, POKE.

DEF SNG

Type of keyword: Statement

Define single (DEF SNG) allows you to define a variable as a single-precision type. Computers that allow definition of variable types usually allow the declaration of integer, single or double precision, and string variable types. On most systems, failure to define a variable usually defaults it to single precision. Double precision allows greater accuracy, while integer variables use the least amount of memory. Once variables are declared, normally all variables beginning with the specified letter will be of the type defined. If you receive an error message, you may have specified an incorrect variable type, as in DEF SNG A$.

Typical syntax:

```
DEF SNG X
DEF SNG A, B, C
```

See also DEF DBL, DEF INT, DEF STR.

DEF STR

Type of keyword: Statement

Define string (DEF STR) allows you to define a variable as a string type. Computers that allow definition of variable types usually allow the declaration of integer, single or double precision, and string variable types. On most systems, failure to define a variable usually defaults it to single precision. Double precision allows greater accuracy, while integer variables use the least amount of memory. Once variables are declared, normally all variables beginning with the specified letter will be of the type defined. If you receive an error message, you may have defined the variable previously.

Typical syntax:

```
DEF STR X
DEF STR A, B, C
```

See also DEF DBL, DEF INT, DEF SNG.

DEF USR

Type of keyword: Command, Statement

The USR function allows transfer of BASIC data into machine language subroutines. The starting location of the machine language routine is specified in the DEF USR statement. (*See* USR.) In the example below, the location of a machine language routine is specified as 32000. Normally, the argument can be a variable or a constant, as can the memory location. The argument within parentheses specifies which USR routine is being called. In many systems, 10 or more routines may be defined at the beginning of the program. The USR argument determines which routine is called. If DEF USR returns an error, you may have specified a memory location that is out of range or nonexistent.

Typical syntax:

```
DEF USR(1) = 32000
```

See also CALL, USR.

DEG

Type of keyword: Command, Statement

The DEG statement is used to set BASIC math functions, such as SIN, ARC, ATN, and so on, to degree mode. This mode allows output of data to be in degree format. To return to radian format, use the command RAD. Normally, DEG does not return an error message.

Typical syntax:

```
DEG
```

See also RAD.

DEL

Type of keyword: Command, Statement

The DEL command will allow you to delete program lines in most BASIC programs. Most computers have several options to DEL. Here is a list of the most common ones:

DEL - deletes all lines in program.
DEL ln deletes the line number specified.
DEL - ln deletes all lines up to and including ln.
DEL ln - deletes all lines from ln to end of program.
DEL ln-ln deletes all lines between lines specified.

Some versions of BASIC allow a comma instead of a dash with the above options. If DEL returns an error, you may have specified nonexistent line numbers or you may not have specified a line.

Typical syntax:

```
DEL-
DEL 10-
DEL-100
DEL 100-150
DEL 100, 120
```

See also DELETE.

DELETE

Type of keyword: Command, Statement

DELETE will allow you to delete program lines in BASIC programs. There are several options to DELETE. Here is a list of the most common ones:

DELETE - deletes all lines in program.

DELETE ln deletes the line specified.

DELETE - ln deletes all lines up to and including ln.

DELETE ln - deletes all lines from ln to the end of the program.

DELETE ln - ln deletes all lines between the lines specified.

Some versions of BASIC allow a comma instead of or in addition to a dash with the above options. If DELETE returns an error, you may have specified nonexistent line numbers or an out-of-range number.

Typical syntax:

```
DELETE-
DELETE 10-
DELETE -100
DELETE 100-200
DELETE 10, 200
```

See also DEL.

DELETE filename

Type of keyword: Command, Statement

DELETE in the filename format is used to remove a file from a listing in the disk directory. Note that most systems don't actually destroy the file, but remove all reference to it in the catalog. If a new file is saved, it will then be saved over the old file, thus finally destroying it. In the second example, volume, slot, and drive number options are shown. If an error message is returned, you may have specified an incorrect or nonexistent filename or option. On many systems the filename must be in quotation marks.

Typical syntax:

```
DELETE HELLO
DELETE PROGRAM, 1, 6, 2
DELETE "PROGMAC"
```

See also DESTROY, ERA, KILL.

DESTROY

Type of keyword: Command, Statement

DESTROY is used when you wish to remove reference to a specific file in a disk directory. Any valid filename is accepted. In the example below, the file named TEMP is removed from the disk. If DESTROY returns an error, you may have specified an improper or nonexistent filename, or the file may be write-protected.

Typical syntax:

```
DESTROY TEMP
```

See also DELETE filename, ERA, KILL.

DIM

Type of keyword: Statement

ANSI

DIM stands for dimension and reserves memory space for a numeric or string array. DIM A (100) reserves 100 variables from A (1) to A (100). Many machines will also allow a zero element, A (0), for a total of 101 variables in our example. String arrays may also be dimensioned on many computers. Some computers dimension only the length of a string, while others treat string arrays like numeric arrays, able to store tables of strings. Most BASICs allow multiple-dimensioned arrays, often called matrices. These arrays have both a column and a row; for example, DIM A (10, 10) reserves a 10 (or 11) column and row table. Many computers also allow multidimensioning above 2; for example, DIM A (10, 10, 10). A default value of 10 is reserved on many machines if the DIM statement is not used. Common error messages encountered include dimensioning arrays too large to fit in memory capacity and redimensioning arrays. An array can only be dimensioned once in a program unless the redimension is preceded by a CLEAR statement.

Typical syntax:

```
DIM L(20)
DIM A$(50)
DIM X(50), Y(50), Z$(100)
```

See also PARAM.

DIR

Type of keyword: Command, Statement

DIR accesses and displays a disk or I/O directory. An optional drive or path number may be allowed, which will specify which device to use. Some computers use a letter rather than a number, as in the third example. Normally, DIR will not return an error message unless the drive or path number is invalid.

Typical syntax:

```
DIR
DIR1
DIR B:
```

See also CATALOG, FILES.

DISPLAY

Type of keyword: Command, Statement

DISPLAY is used to print strings or numbers on the screen in TI BASIC. DISPLAY cannot print to any device except the screen. All normal PRINT options are available with DISPLAY.

Typical syntax:

```
DISPLAY L$, X;Y
```

See also PRINT.

DLOAD

Type of keyword: Command, Statement

DLOAD is used on the TRS–80 Color Computer to download a BASIC file from a host computer. Two baud rates can be specified: 300 and 1200. The number specified will set the baud rate.

0 = 300 BAUD
1 = 1200 BAUD

In the example below, the file named "filename" will be downloaded at 1200 baud. If an error message is returned, you may have specified an improper filename or out-of-range baud specifier.

Typical syntax:

```
DLOAD "FILENAME", 1
```

DLOADM

Type of keyword: Command, Statement

DLOADM is used on the TRS–80 Color Computer to download a machine language file from a host computer. Two baud rates can be specified: 300 and 1200. The number specified will set the baud rate.

0 = 300 BAUD

1 = 1200 BAUD

In the example below, the file named "filename" will be downloaded at 1200 baud. If an error message is returned, you may have specified an improper filename or out-of-range baud specifier.

Typical syntax:

```
DLOADM "FILENAME", 1
```

DO

See WHILE–DO.

DRAW

Type of keyword: Command, Statement

DRAW executes a shape defined from a shape table. In the first example below, shape number 3 is drawn starting at coordinates 20, 30, on a high-resolution screen. In the second example, DRAW is used to execute a shape at the last coordinates specified. Color, rotation, and scale must be predefined, and the shape table must be loaded. If DRAW returns an error, you may have specified out-of-range coordinates or shape table data.

Typical syntax:

```
DRAW 3 AT 20, 30
DRAW 24
```

See also MDRAW, XDRAW.

DRAW str

Type of keyword: Statement

The DRAW statement is a graphics command that allows execution of graphics using strings. The string must contain starting and ending points, and can specify scale, color, and relative distance. Other options include execution of substrings, blank lines, and nonupdated lines, and begin from prespecified locations. Strings can be variables or constants. In the first example, a small square will be drawn near the center of the screen. Some systems use a number instead of a string, such as found in the LINE command. If DRAW returns an error, you may have specified an improper character in the string. An error message will also be returned if screen coordinates are out of range.

Typical syntax:

```
DRAW "BM128, 96; U25; R25; D25; L25"
DRAW L$
```

See also DRAWTO, GLINE, HLIN, LINE, MDRAW, RDRAW, VLIN.

DRAWTO

Type of keyword: Command, Statement

The DRAWTO statement is a graphics command that allows execution of lines on the display. Numbers can be variables or constants. In the first example, a line will be drawn from the last PLOT or DRAWTO statement to position (10, 15). If DRAWTO returns an error, you may have specified screen coordinates that are out of range.

Typical syntax:

```
DRAWTO 10, 15
DRAWTO X, Y
```

See also DRAW str, GLINE, HLIN, LINE, MDRAW, RDRAW, VLIN.

DRIVE

Type of keyword: Command, Statement

DRIVE changes the default drive to the specified drive number. Upon initialization, one drive is automatically chosen. With DRIVE, you can select another drive. Many computers have no equivalent command; however, when you specify a file read or write, or directory access to a drive other than the default drive, the newly specified drive becomes the default drive. If DRIVE returns an error, you may have specified a nonexistent or unready drive number.

Typical syntax:

```
DRIVE 1
```

DSKI$

Type of keyword: Command, Statement

DSKI$ reads a defined track and sector. The command bypasses the disk filing system, allowing normally inaccessible tracks to be read. In the example below, A$ and B$ contain the first and second 128 bytes, respectively, of track 1, sector 18, on the disk in drive zero. All numbers can be variable or constant, but the strings must be variables rather than constants, since they will have data placed in them. If DSKI$ returns an error, you may have specified an incorrect parameter.

Typical syntax:

```
DSKI$ 0, 1, 18, A$, B$
```

See also DSKO$.

DSKINI

Type of keyword: Command

DSKINI formats a disk in the specified drive number. The formatting process divides a soft-sectored disk into tracks and sectors. If DSKINI returns an error, you may have specified an incorrect drive number.

Typical syntax:

```
DSKINI 0
```

See also FORMAT, INIT.

DSKO$

Type of keyword: Command, Statement

DSKO$ writes a defined track and sector to a disk. The command bypasses the disk filing system, allowing normally inaccessible tracks to be written. In the example below, A$ and B$ contain up to 128 bytes each, which will be placed into track 1, sector 18, on the disk in drive zero. All numbers can be variable or constant; strings may contain less than 128 bytes each and may be expressed as variables or constants. If an error message is returned, you may have specified an improper parameter. Caution must be used when using this command. If you overwrite end-of-file or directory information, you may destroy access to part or all of the disk.

Typical syntax:

```
DSKO$ 0, 1, 18, A$, B$
```

See also DSKI$.

E

EDIT line number

Type of keyword: Command

EDIT is used on many different computers to modify an existing program line. There are many variations of the EDIT command. Check your operation manual for specific details on your editor, if available. Most line editors allow insertion and deletion of characters, character search, and replace. If EDIT returns an error message, you may have specified an improper line number.

Typical syntax:

```
EDIT 10
```

ELLIPSE

Type of keyword: Statement

The ELLIPSE command is used to draw a flattened or lengthened circle on the graphics display device. Since an ellipse is a circle with more than one radius, two radii must be specified in the command. In the first example below, a circle is drawn with a horizontal radius of 1 and a vertical radius of 0.5. A pattern parameter is allowed, which fills the ellipse with the pattern specified by the pattern number. If ELLIPSE returns an error, you may have specified illegal radius range or out-of-range coordinates.

Typical syntax:

```
ELLIPSE 1, .5
ELLIPSE 1, 2, 200
```

See also CIRCLE, PIESLICE.

ELSE
See IF–THEN.

END

Type of keyword: Statement

ANSI

The END statement is used to stop program execution. In many cases, this must be the last line of the program. On most micros, the END statement is optional. END may be used just ahead of subroutines so that program control doesn't start executing a RETURN without a GOSUB statement. Normally, END doesn't return an error message.

Typical syntax:

```
END
```

See also STOP.

ENDEXIT

Type of keyword: Statement

ENDEXIT is used to terminate an EXIT clause from a FOR–NEXT loop or other loop construct. In the example below, if L is greater than 10, then control will leave the loop. Normally, ENDEXIT doesn't return an error message.

Typical syntax:

```
EXITIF L>10 THEN PRINT "L IS GREATER THAN
10"
ENDEXIT
```

See also ENDIF, ENDLOOP, ENDWHILE, EXITIF, LOOP.

ENDIF

Type of keyword: Statement

ENDIF is used to terminate multiple-line IF–THEN statements. The program listing below is an example of how to use the ENDIF statement. Upon execution, if A is equal to 7, then the computer will execute line 20; otherwise control will go to line 40, which ends the program. If ENDIF returns an error message, you may not have specified an IF statement.

Typical syntax:

```
10 IF A = 7 THEN PRINT A
20 PRINT "NUMBER A IS EQUAL TO 7"
30 ENDIF
40 END
```

See also ENDEXIT, ENDLOOP, ENDWHILE, EXITIF, LOOP.

ENDLOOP

Type of keyword: Statement

ENDLOOP is used in conjunction with LOOP to set up a loop that allows testing within any part of the loop. ENDEXIT and EXITIF provide the test structure. The example below demonstrates how the loop structure is set up. If ENDLOOP returns an error, you may not have specified a loop beginning.

Typical syntax:

```
INPUT X
LOOP
EXITIF X <0
PRINT "X IS LESS THAN ZERO"
ENDEXIT
PRINT "X IS GREATER THAN OR EQUAL TO ZERO"
X = X-1
ENDLOOP
```

See also ENDEXIT, ENDIF, ENDWHILE, EXITIF, LOOP.

ENDWHILE

Type of keyword: Statement

ENDWHILE is used to terminate multiple-line WHILE–DO statements. The program listing below is an example of how to use the ENDWHILE statement. Upon execution, if A is equal to 7, then the computer will execute line 20; otherwise control will go to line 40, which ends the program. If ENDWHILE returns an error message, you may not have specified a WHILE–DO statement.

Typical syntax:

```
WHILE X>Y DO
Y = Y + 1
PRINT Y
ENDWHILE
```

See also ENDEXIT, ENDIF, ENDLOOP, EXITIF, LOOP.

EOF

Type of keyword: Statement

EOF is a file related command. It is used to test whether you have reached the end of a disk or tape data file. Normally, the program tests for EOF (true) before trying to input more data from the buffer. In the example below, if EOF is true, program control goes to line 100, where presumably the file is closed, and program execution continues. Errors related to EOF are usually caused by specifying an incorrect or nonexistent file buffer number.

Typical syntax:

```
50 IF EOF (1) THEN 100
```

See also LOF.

EQV

Type of keyword: Operator

EQV is an operator used to denote equivalence. If two variables are tested for equivalence, EQV returns true if the two items are equal; otherwise EQV returns false. In the example below, if the variables A and B are of equal value, the computer will print 1; otherwise it will print zero.

Typical syntax:

```
A EQV B
```

ERA

Type of keyword: Command, Statement

ERA is used to delete a file from the disk directory. It also allows reallocation of the file space to free disk memory. If ERA returns an error, you may have specified a nonexistent file, an incorrect drive, or an incorrect file extension.

Typical syntax:

```
ERA FILENAME.EXT
```

See also DELETE, DESTROY, KILL.

ERASE

Type of keyword: Statement

The ERASE statement is used to delete an array or arrays from memory when they are no longer needed. ERASE allows you to release a previously dimensioned variable for reuse. You may also extend memory capacity for other variables by erasing arrays that are no longer being used. In some computers, ERASE is used to remove a program from memory. If ERASE returns an error, you may have incorrectly specified a variable.

Typical syntax:

```
ERASE X
ERASE A, B
```

See also CLEAR, NEW.

ERL

Type of keyword: Statement

The ERL assignment allows you to handle errors from within a BASIC program. In the example below, the variable A will contain the line number that contains an error that has occurred. Once the line number is known, the program can branch to the proper error-handling routine.

Typical syntax:

```
A = ERL
```

See also ERR.

ERR

Type of keyword: Statement

The ERR assignment allows you to handle errors from within a BASIC program. In the example below, the variable A will contain the code number of an error that has occurred. Once the error code is known, the program can branch to the proper error-handling routine.

Typical syntax:

```
A = ERR
```

See also ERL.

ERROR

Type of keyword: Command, Statement

The ERROR assignment allows you to simulate the occurrence of an error in a program. You may also define your own error messages. In the example below, the computer will print the error message associated with error number 12. ERROR can be used to test the operation of error-handling routines in your programs. Usually, the error number must be an integer between 1 and 255, inclusive.

Typical syntax:

```
ERROR 12
```

See also ERL, ERR, ON ERR GOTO, ON ERROR GOTO.

ERRSET

Type of keyword: Statement

ERRSET is used to specify the location and handling variables of an error-trapping routine. In the first example, the program will, upon occurrence of an error, go to line 10000 and begin execution. The variables LI and ER contain the values of the line number that contains an error and the number of the error itself, respectively. In the second example, the error-trapping routine is disabled. If ERRSET returns an error, you may have specified an out-of-range line number or incorrect variable type.

Typical syntax:

```
ERRSET 10000, LI, ER
ERRSET
```

See also ERL, ERR, ON ERR GOTO, ON ERROR GOTO.

EXAM

Type of keyword: Function

EXAM is used to examine the contents of the specified memory location. In the example below, the variable X will contain the data, in decimal format, of the contents of memory location 65535. If EXAM returns an error, you may have specified an out-of-range or nonexistent memory location.

Typical syntax:

```
EXAM {65535}
```

See also PEEK.

EXEC

Type of keyword: Command, Statement

EXEC is a system-specific command that executes a machine language program previously loaded. Address is optional and, if not used, the last specified address is used. In the example below, after loading the machine language program, it is automatically executed from a BASIC program. EXEC returns an error message if no address has been specified.

Typical syntax:

```
40 LOADM "MONITOR"=:= EXEC
```

See also BRUN, CALL, SYS.

EXEC filename

Type of keyword: Command

EXEC is a disk BASIC command used to execute a text or data file. The data file contains BASIC-like commands that would normally be input from the keyboard. EXEC allows multiple programs and processes to be run from a single utility and provides a turnkey system. A position option is included that operates within the file in a similar fashion to the disk BASIC POSITION command. In the second example, position, volume, slot, and drive number options are shown. If an error message is returned, you may have specified an incorrect or nonexistent filename or option.

Typical syntax:

```
EXEC TEXTDATA
EXEC FILE, R29, 1, 6, 2
```

EXIT

Type of keyword: Statement

EXIT is used when you wish to terminate a FOR–NEXT loop before the loop has terminated on its own. The new execution start line is specified. In the example below, control will resume with line 1000 if X is equal to 50. The new control point must be outside the loop. EXIT must only be used when in a loop. If EXIT returns an error, you may have specified an out-of-range or nonexistent line number, or no loop was being executed.

Typical syntax:

```
IF X = 50 THEN EXIT 1000
```

EXITIF

Type of keyword: Statement

EXITIF is used to begin an EXIT clause in a FOR–NEXT loop or other loop construct. In the example below, if L is greater than

10, then control will leave the loop. EXITIF statements must be terminated with an ENDEXIT statement.

Typical syntax:

```
EXITIF L>10 THEN PRINT "L IS GREATER THAN
10"
ENDEXIT
```

See also ENDEXIT, ENDIF, ENDLOOP, ENDWHILE, LOOP.

EXP

Type of keyword: Function

ANSI

EXP returns the natural exponential of the specified number. The number can be a constant or a variable, and many BASICs allow math operations within the argument. In the example below, L will contain the exponential of variable X. If an error message is returned, you may have specified an out-of-range number.

Typical syntax:

```
L = EXP {X}
```

F

FALSE

Type of keyword: Function

This function will always return the equivalent of logic zero when used. In the example below, X$ will contain the message "FALSE." Normally, FALSE will not return an error message.

Typical syntax:

```
X$ = FALSE
```

See also TRUE.

FAST

Type of keyword: Command, Statement

FAST is a system-specific command that puts the Timex/Sinclair computer into a high-speed mode. When placed in fast mode, the computer does not update the screen display so that maximum effort can be placed into operating on data. Use SLOW to return to normal mode. Normally, FAST will not return an error message.

Typical syntax:

```
FAST
```

See also SLOW.

FIELD

Type of keyword: Statement

FIELD is a disk BASIC file statement used with random access disk files. FIELD organizes a file buffer into data blocks. In the example below, buffer number 1 is divided into name, address, city, and state strings. The numbers indicate the number of bytes to be reserved in the field. If FIELD returns an error, you may have specified a greater number of bytes in the field than there is room for in the buffer. For example, if the buffer is 25 characters long and the total of field bytes reserved is greater than 25, an error message will result.

Typical syntax:

```
FIELD #1, 25 AS N$, 25 AS A$, 15 AS C$, 2 AS S$
```

FILE

Type of keyword: Function

FILE is used to determine the filetype of a disk file. In the example below, the computer will return a number corresponding to the filetype of the file specified in the argument. If an improper filename or nonexistent file is specified, a −1 is returned. Filetypes include BASIC files, ASCII or TEXT files, binary files, and so on.

Typical syntax:

```
X = FILE "FILESPEC"
```

FILES

Type of keyword: Command, Statement

The FILES command is a disk BASIC command that reserves buffer memory space. In many systems, there are three simultaneous files available when the computer is powered up. If you want to reserve more or fewer files, thus expanding or contracting memory buffer space, issue the FILES command. An option with the FILES command is the number of bytes reserved in each file buffer. In the first example the computer contains the default buffer value, while in the second example each buffer is defined to be 250 bytes in length. If FILES returns an error, you may have specified a total number of files that is out of range of the system, or you may have tried to reserve more file space than you have memory for. Check FILES filename for machines that use FILES to display an index of files.

Typical syntax:

```
FILES 3
FILES 3, 250
```

See also FILES filename, MAXFILES.

FILES filename

Type of keyword: Command

FILES is used to display filenames on a selected disk. If the filename is omitted, all files will be displayed. Several options allow a wildcard match. In the first example, all files with the extension /BIN will be listed. The second example will display all files containing AB in the first two character positions.

Typical syntax:

```
FILES "*/BIN"
FILES "AB?.*"
```

See also CAT, CATALOG, DIR.

FILL

Type of keyword: Command, Statement

FILL is used to put a byte of data into a single memory location. The location must be RAM, and the location and number specified can be constants or variables. In the example below, the number 100 will be placed in location 16314. If an error message is returned, you may have specified an out-of-range or nonexistent memory location.

Typical syntax:

```
FILL 16314, 100
```

See also POKE.

FIX

Type of keyword: Function

FIX truncates a number to the decimal point. Though similar to the INT function, FIX truncates the number instead of rounding it down. In the first example, L will be equal to 10. In the second example, L is equal to −9 rather than −10 as it would be in the INT function. If FIX returns an error, you may have specified a number that is out of range of your interpreter.

Typical syntax:

```
L = FIX (10.93)
L = FIX (-9.1)
```

See also INT.

FLASH

Type of keyword: Command, Statement

FLASH is used to cause the video text display to shift between normal and reverse video. Upon execution of the FLASH command, all text printed on the screen will flash. In the example below, HELLO will flash; FRIEND will not. To return to normal video, use NORMAL. Any print statements still on the screen written while FLASH was in effect will continue to flash. Normally, FLASH will not return an error message.

Typical syntax:

```
10 FLASH
20 PRINT "HELLO"
30 NORMAL
40 PRINT "FRIEND"
```

FLOAT

Type of keyword: Function

The FLOAT function will convert a variable to a real type. A real variable contains a floating decimal point. In the example below, the integer variable X will be converted to a real variable and stored in Y. If FLOAT returns an error, you may have specified an improper variable type.

Typical syntax:

```
Y = FLOAT {X%}
```

FN
See DEF FN.

FNEND

Type of keyword: Statement

FNEND is used to complete the definition of a multiple-line function. Some computers that allow DEF FN can allow the definition of the function to use more than one line number.

Upon completion of the definition, an FNEND statement indicates that the definition is complete. The FNEND command must be preceded by a RETURN from function definition command. (*See* RETURN.) If FNEND returns an error, you may have placed the FNEND statement on the same line as DEF FN or tried to execute the FNEND statement.

Typical syntax:

```
10 DEF FNA{X}
20 X = INT {RND {0}*100}
30 RETURN X
40 FNEND
```

See also DEF FN.

FOR–TO

Type of keyword: Statement

ANSI

FOR in conjunction with TO creates a loop that executes from the lower number specified to the upper. In the example below, the statement between the FOR and NEXT statements will be executed until the variable L is greater than 10. There are many variations available in most BASICs. In many BASICs, it is not required to specify the variable in the next statement. Another variation is the STEP command, which allows the loop variable to increment by a number other than 1. STEP also allows a decrementing loop, by specifying a negative number in the STEP statement. In the second example, the variable X will increment by 2 until it reaches 34, when it will exit the loop and continue with the statement immediately following the NEXT. The FOR statement usually does not return an error; however, improper use of the NEXT statement can cease program execution.

Typical syntax:

```
10 FOR L = 1 TO 10
20 PRINT L
30 NEXT L
```

```
10 FOR X = 10 TO 32 STEP 2
20 PRINT X
30 NEXT X
```

See also LOOP, REPEAT–UNTIL, WHILE–DO, WHILE–WEND.

FRE

Type of keyword: Function

FRE is used to determine the amount of available memory remaining for program and data use. In the example below, L will contain the amount of free memory left. The argument inside the parentheses is unimportant but must be legal and is usually a zero. The value returned by FRE will be affected by the amount of memory reserved for strings and machine language programs. In addition to the first example, some computers use FRE with a string variable to initiate a string reorganization routine. The syntax is displayed in the second example.

Typical syntax:

```
L = FRE (0)
FRE (Z$)
```

See also FREE, MEM.

FREE

Type of keyword: Function

FREE is a disk BASIC command that calculates the amount of free file space available on the disk in the drive number specified. In the example below, the amount of file space on the disk in drive zero will be printed. In most disk systems, the total number of drives must be 4 or less. If FREE returns an error, you may have specified an out-of-range drive number. In addition, many systems use FREE to determine the amount of free memory available to BASIC.

Typical syntax:

```
PRINT FREE (0)
```

See also FRE, MEM.

G

GCLS

Type of keyword: Command, Statement

GCLS is used on Epson computers to clear graphics from the screen. GCLS differs from CLS in that any text that was on the screen remains there. GCLS will not normally return an error message.

Typical syntax:

```
GCLS
```

See also CLS, PCLS.

GET

Type of keyword: Statement

GET is a disk-oriented command in random access disk file systems. The numbers specify the buffer number and record number, respectively. The numbers can be constants or variables. The buffer number must match the file buffer designated in the OPEN statement. If the record number is omitted, the next record in the file is accessed. In the example below, record number 15 is read from the disk and placed in disk buffer number 1. If an error message is returned, you may have specified an incorrect buffer number or a number greater than the last record in the file. Some systems allow the use of a number that is called a unit number. The unit can be any type of I/O device.

Typical syntax:

```
GET #1, 15
```

GET coordinates

Type of keyword: Command, Statement

GET is a graphics command used to store the contents of a screen display for later use. The coordinates specified are outer boundaries of a rectangle containing the screen details to be stored. The information is stored in an array that must be dimensioned to the proper size before using GET. A graphics option can be used that allows modification of the stored array when it is placed on the screen. In the example below, the array L will contain screen information from the rectangle specified. The G indicates use of the graphics option. If GET returns an error message, you may have specified out-of-range coordinates or you may not have dimensioned a large enough array.

Typical syntax:

```
GET (100, 90) - (110, 100), V, G
```

See also PUT.

GET str

Type of keyword: Function

GET is used to input a single keystroke from the keyboard. Program execution stops, and usually a block cursor is printed indicating that an input is desired. When you strike the key, the value of the key struck is stored in the string specified. In the example below, L$ will contain the string value of the key pressed. GET cannot be used in immediate mode but otherwise will not usually return an error.

Typical syntax:

```
GET L$
```

See also CALL CHAR, GETKEY, INCHAR$, INKEY$, INPUT, INPUT$, LINE INPUT.

GIN

Type of keyword: Statement

GIN is a graphics-oriented statement that allows the program to locate the current graphics cursor position. The current X and Y coordinates are stored in the variables following the GIN command. In the example below, horizontal cursor position is stored in variable H, while vertical position is stored in variable V. Variables may be any legal numeric format. If GIN returns an error, you may have specified an illegal variable definition or type.

Typical syntax:

```
GIN H, V
```

GINIT

Type of keyword: Statement

GINIT is used to initialize and format graphics display characteristics. The four functions GINIT sets up are viewport size, window area, cursor position, and rotation angle. GINIT is used when you wish to start working with a new screen. Normally, GINIT will not return an error message.

Typical syntax:

```
GINIT
```

GLINE

Type of keyword: Statement

GLINE is a graphics command that will draw a line from one coordinate to another. In addition, it updates the cursor position to the end of the newly completed line. Coordinates may be expressed as either numeric constants or variables. In the first example below, a line will be drawn from location (10, 20) to (30, 50), The second example demonstrates use of a pattern number. If GLINE returns an error, you may have specified out-of-range coordinates or pattern number.

Typical syntax:

```
GLINE 10, 20, 30, 50
GLINE A, B, X1, Y1, 100
```

See also DRAW str, DRAWTO, HLIN, LINE, RLINE, VLIN.

GO
See GOSUB, GO TO.

GOFF

Type of keyword: Statement

GOFF is used to inhibit data display on the video display device. Once the display is turned off, it can be turned on again by GON or TEXT commands. Normally, GOFF will not return an error message.

Typical syntax:

```
GOFF
```

See also GON, GR, HGR, SCREEN.

GON

Type of keyword: Statement

GON is used to enable the graphics display device. When used in conjunction with GOFF, graphics displays may be updated while the screen is off and then turned on again for display. Normally, GON will not return an error message.

Typical syntax:

```
GON
```

See also GOFF, GR, HGR, SCREEN.

GOSUB

Type of keyword: Statement

ANSI

GOSUB is used to send program control to a subroutine. A subroutine is a block of code that is usually executed more than once in a program. With GOSUB, you may use that routine from any location in your program. All valid subroutines must end in a RETURN statement. RETURN sends program control to the statement immediately following the GOSUB. In the example below, program control is sent to line 100. The subroutine is executed, and BASIC returns to line 20. If GOSUB returns an error, you have probably specified a nonexistent line number.

Typical syntax:

```
10 GOSUB 100
20 END
100 PRINT "HELLO"
110 RETURN
```

See also GOTO, ON–GOSUB, RETURN.

GOTO

Type of keyword: Statement

ANSI

GOTO sends program control to the line number specified. Execution continues from that point on. In the example below, the program continues at line 100. If GOTO returns an error, you have probably specified a nonexistent or out-of-range line number.

Typical syntax:

```
GOTO 100
```

See also GOSUB, ON–GOTO.

GPRINT

Type of keyword: Statement

GPRINT is used to print text on a graphics screen display. All normal print options are allowed, and the printing starts at the current position of the graphics cursor. See PRINT for the list of printing options.

Typical syntax:

```
GPRINT "HELLO"
GPRINT "THIS IS AN EXAMPLE"; A$
GPRINT "NUMBER"; X, A(X)
```

See also PRINT.

GR

Type of keyword: Command, Statement

GR is a graphics command that sets the computer to low-resolution graphics mode. It will clear the screen and enable a low-resolution graphics display. On the Apple II computer, GR will allow four lines of text at the screen bottom. The first example demonstrates Apple syntax. On the Atari series, the screen will allow mixed text and graphics block characters. The second example demonstrates syntax for the Atari, which calls graphics screen zero. A normal text window is allowed by using the syntax in the last example. Normally, GR will not return an error unless you specify an out-of-range number.

Typical syntax:

```
10 GR
10 GR.0
10 GR.1+16
```

See also GOFF, GON, GRAPHICS, HYBRID, PCLS, PMODE.

GRAPHICS

Type of keyword: Statement

GRAPHICS is used to initialize and enter the graphics mode. The screen will clear and initialize internal graphics variables. The resolution available is 160 × 120 pixels. Normally, GRAPHICS will not return an error.

Typical syntax:

```
GRAPHICS
```

See also GR, HGR, SCREEN.

H

HCOLOR

Type of keyword: Command, Statement

HCOLOR is a high-resolution graphics color statement. In the example below, HCOLOR sets the next color to be plotted to green. Changing HCOLOR will change the next color to be plotted, while leaving previously plotted colors the same. If HCOLOR returns an error, you may have specified an out-of-range color number.

Typical syntax:

```
HCOLOR = 1
```

See also COLOR.

HEX$

Type of keyword: Function

HEX$ is a conversion function that converts a decimal number to hexadecimal format. In the example below, L$ will be equal to the hexadecimal value of 16 decimal. The argument may be a constant or a variable, and usually math operations are allowed within the argument. Since L$ is actually a string, math functions cannot usually be applied to the string. Some computers allow hex numbers instead of decimal numbers by including a hex marker. For example, in &HCD12, the hex marker &H notifies the computer that the number following is in hexadecimal format. If HEX$ returns an error, you may have specified a number that is out of range of the interpreter.

Typical syntax:

```
L$ = HEX$ (16)
```

HGR

Type of keyword: Command, Statement

HGR is a graphics command that sets the high-resolution graphics mode of the computer. HGR leaves four lines of text visible at the bottom of the screen, unless specified otherwise with a POKE 49234, 0, which leaves a full graphics page. In the second example, page 2 of the graphics memory is displayed. Normally, an error message will not occur; however, the high-resolution graphics screen may appear if you should accidentally define a variable such as HGROW = 125.

Typical syntax:

```
HGR
HGR2
```

See also GOFF, GON, GRAPHICS, PMODE, SCREEN.

HIMEM:

Type of keyword: Command, Statement

HIMEM: tells BASIC the highest available memory for use in a BASIC program. It is used to protect memory for the disk operating system, high-resolution graphics screen, or any machine language routines. In the example below, memory above 32 kilobytes is reserved for a machine language routine. If HIMEM: returns an error, you may have specified an out-of-range argument.

Typical syntax:

```
HIMEM: 32767
```

See also CLEAR, MEMSET.

HLIN

Type of keyword: Command, Statement

HLIN will draw a horizontal line at the appropriate position specified. In the example below, a line will be drawn from pixel 20 to pixel 40 on row 30. On a coordinate system, the line would be drawn from position (20, 30) to (40, 30). If HLIN returns an error, you may have specified a number that is out of range.

Typical syntax:

```
HLIN 20, 40 AT 30
```

See also DRAW str, DRAWTO, GLINE, LINE, VLIN.

HOME

Type of keyword: Command, Statement

HOME clears the video screen of information and returns the cursor to the upper left corner. Normally, no error message will be returned.

Typical syntax:

```
HOME
```

See also CLEAR, CLR, CLS.

HPLOT

Type of keyword: Command, Statement

HPLOT places dots and lines in high-resolution graphics modes. The color is specified from a previous HCOLOR statement. In the first example, a dot is plotted at pixel (20, 40). The second example plots a line from (20, 40) to (50, 60). If the first coordinate is omitted, as in the third example, a line will be plotted from the last dot previously specified to the last coordinate pair. The color of the line will assume the color of the last dot plotted. If HPLOT returns an error, you have probably specified coordinates that are out of range of the system.

Typical syntax:

```
HPLOT 20, 40
HPLOT 20, 40 TO 50, 60
HPLOT TO 20, 20
```

See also DRAW str, DRAWTO, LINE, PSET, SET.

HTAB

Type of keyword: Command, Statement

HTAB is used to position the cursor on the horizontal line. In the example below, the next print will occur at column 10. If HTAB returns an error, you have probably specified a number that is out of range.

Typical syntax:

```
HTAB 10
```

See also CALL HCHAR, CALL VCHAR, CSRLIN, LOCATE, POSITION, PRINT@, SPC, TAB.

HYBRID

Type of keyword: Statement

HYBRID is a command used to set up and initialize the graphics screen and allow for four lines of text. When this mode is used, graphics statements may be used in the upper screen area, while text is displayed in the bottom four lines of the screen. Graphics statements that reference the bottom of the screen are acted upon; however, the display is covered up by the text. Normally, HYBRID will not return an error message.

Typical syntax:

```
HYBRID
```

See also GR.

I

IF–THEN

Type of keyword: Statement

ANSI

IF–THEN is the most commonly used decision-making statement in BASIC. There are several variations of IF–THEN. In the first example below, if the variable L is greater than 10, then program control is sent to line 100. When a condition of the IF–THEN is met, the condition is said to be true. If the condition is false, control proceeds to the line number following the IF–THEN statement. In the second example, the message "IMPROPER OPTION" is printed, and the GOTO following the colon is executed if the condition is true. If not, the print statement and GOTO are both ignored as control falls to the next line number. An option allowed by many interpreters is ELSE. The third example demonstrates that the ELSE statement is executed if the condition is false. In many BASICs, THEN is optional; for example, IF A < 2 GOTO 50. Another variation is IF A < 2 THEN 50, which means the same thing. An error message will result if branching sends control to a nonexistent line number.

Typical syntax:

```
IF L>10 THEN GOTO 100
40 IF M>8 THEN PRINT "IMPROPER OPTION":
GOTO 20
150 IF X<10 THEN GOTO 200 ELSE PRINT "YOUR
CHOICE": GOTO 100
```

IN #

Type of keyword: Command, Statement

IN # identifies the slot from which the next input will occur. The peripheral in the slot will provide input until the command IN # 0. At that point, input control returns to the keyboard. In the example below, the peripheral in slot 2 will provide input. If IN # returns an error, you may have specified a number that is out of range.

Typical syntax:

```
IN # 2
```

INCHAR$

Type of keyword: Function

INCHAR$ is used to scan the keyboard looking for a keypress. As can be seen by the examples, INCHAR$ must be followed by a numeric expression. A zero references to the system keyboard, while a 1 references to the remote terminal keyboard. INCHAR$ stops program operation while it waits for a keypress, and the contents of the key pressed will be stored in the assigned variable. Only one character will be saved. Normally, INCHAR$ will not return an error message unless the variable is an illegal type.

Typical syntax:

```
X$ = INCHAR$ (0)
Y$ = INCHAR$ (1)
```

See also CALL CHAR, GET str, INKEY$, INPUT, INPUT$.

INIT

Type of keyword: Command

INIT initializes a disk and formats its tracks and sectors. In the first example, the disk is initialized with the program HELLO. HELLO will automatically load and execute when the disk is booted. In the second example, the options to INIT are shown. PROGRAM is being initialized, and the disk volume, slot, and drive number are specified. If INIT returns an error, you may have specified an improper filename or out-of-range option.

Typical syntax:

```
INIT HELLO
INIT PROGRAM, 1, 6, 2
```

See also DSKINI, FORMAT.

INKEY$

Type of keyword: Function

INKEY$ scans the keyboard looking for a keypress. If a keypress is found, the specified variable will hold the key pressed. If no key is pressed, a null code is stored in the variable. INKEY$ allows keyboard input without stopping program execution to wait for an ENTER or RETURN key. In most BASICs, INKEY$ scans the keyboard once and continues on. It is possible to stop execution of a program by putting the INKEY$ in a loop until it finds a valid key. See the example below. Normally, INKEY$ will not return an error.

Typical syntax:

```
A$ = INKEY$
100 X$ = INKEY$: IF X$ = "" THEN 100
```

See also CALL KEY, GET str, INCHAR$, INPUT$.

INP

Type of keyword: Function

INP is used to read data contained at an input port. In the example below, variable X will contain the value of data stored at port number 1. If INP returns an error, you may have specified a port number that is out of range of the available ports.

Typical syntax:

```
X = INP (1)
```

INPUT

Type of keyword: Statement

ANSI

INPUT stops program execution and waits for the operator to insert data. The variable specified can be numeric or string. Program execution continues upon receipt of the ENTER or RETURN key. There are several options to INPUT. The first example gathers a numeric variable. A string variable is obtained from the second example. Many BASICs allow multiple-input statements, as in the third example. To use the third option, the operator will separate his or her responses with a comma. Normally, this means that a comma cannot be put into an input statement (unless the entire statement is enclosed in quotes). Another option is the "prompt" statement. Normally, INPUT prints a ? to indicate the fact that the computer is waiting for data. By including a prompt message, the programmer can tell the operator what kind of data is desired. Normally the prompt statement does not require a ?, as the INPUT mark appears automatically after the prompt. There are three common errors relating to the INPUT statement. A typematch error will result if you try to enter string data (such as a letter) for numeric data. Some BASICs automatically print the error message and let you reenter the number without stopping the program. An extra data ignored, or too much data error will occur if a comma or colon is found in an input statement. Normally, program execution will continue using all data up to the delimiter. Delimiters can be entered if the input statement is enclosed in quotes. A long-string error will occur if the input data is too long for the interpreter. In most computers, a maximum of 255 characters is allowed. In many cases, the INPUT errors listed will not stop program execution. Error messages are cryptic to most operators, however, so you should use error trapping to ensure that no incorrect data are included. North Star uses a variation, INPUT1, which outputs no carriage return to the display device. This causes PRINT statements after the input to be displayed immediately after the user's response to the INPUT1 statement.

Typical syntax:

```
INPUT L
INPUT A$
INPUT X, Y
INPUT "PROMPT"; A$
INPUT1 Z$
```

See also CALL KEY, GET, INCHAR$, INKEY$, INPUT #, INPUT$, LINE INPUT.

INPUT #

Type of keyword: Statement

The INPUT # statement is a file-oriented command that inputs data from the buffer number specified. Unlike INPUT, which takes input from the keyboard, this statement takes its input from the buffer number specified. The data in the buffer are assigned to the string or numeric variable specified. In the first example below, L is given the data input from buffer number 1. In the second example, buffer number 2 contains string data that will be assigned to B$. If INPUT # returns an error, you may not have opened the file specified in the buffer number or you may have created a type mismatch by trying to assign string data to a numeric variable.

Typical syntax:

```
INPUT #1, L
INPUT #2, B$
```

See also INPUT, LINE INPUT.

INPUT1
See INPUT.

INPUT$

Type of keyword: Statement

INPUT$ is used to obtain a certain number of characters from the keyboard and assign them to a specified variable. In the first example below, INPUT$ will store the next 10 characters received from the keyboard into A$. If a buffer number is specified, as in the second example, the device associated with that buffer will become the input device.

Typical syntax:

```
A$ = INPUT$ (10)
A$ = INPUT$ (X, #1)
```

See also CALL CHAR, GET, INCHAR$, INKEY$, INPUT, INPUT#.

INSTR

Type of keyword: Function

INSTR is a statement that performs a string search. INSTR returns a number that represents the position within the search string of the first character of the target string. If the number is zero, the target string was not found within the string being searched. The number specifies the position from which the search is to start. If the number is omitted, search begins with the first character. In the first example below, L will be equal to 5, the position of the first letter of the target string. The argument may contain constants or variables. If INSTR returns an error, you may have specified nonexistent strings or a number that is out of range.

Typical syntax:

```
L = INSTR ("JOHNSON", "SON")
A = INSTR (3, A$, B$)
```

See also LEFT$, MID$, POS str, RIGHT$, SUBSTR.

INT

Type of keyword: Function

ANSI

INT converts a number to its integer. The argument can be either a constant or a variable. The INT function does not round a number up, only down. In the examples below, L is 10 and −10. If INT returns an error, you have specified a number too large or too small for the BASIC interpreter to handle.

Typical syntax:

```
L = INT (10.93)
L = INT (-9.1)
```

INVERSE

Type of keyword: Command, Statement

INVERSE reverses the state of the video output at the CRT. INVERSE produces dark letters on a white background. To return to light-on-dark format, use NORMAL.

Typical syntax:

```
INVERSE
```

J

JOYSTK

Type of keyword: Function

JOYSTK reads the horizontal and vertical coordinates of the computer joystick port. The argument specifies horizontal or vertical, left or right reading.

0 = horizontal right
1 = vertical right
2 = horizontal left
3 = vertical left

With the TRS–80 Color Computer, JOYSTK (0) must be read before reading any other parameter. In the example below, L will contain a number between zero and 63, depending upon the horizontal position of the right joystick. If JOYSTK returns an error, you may have specified an out-of-range argument.

Typical syntax:

```
L = JOYSTK (0)
```

See also CALL JOYSTK, PDL.

K

KEY

Type of keyword: Command, Statement

KEY is used to define the special function keys on the keyboard. In the example below, special function key number 3 is being defined as the PRINT command. Once it is defined, when the user presses function key 3, PRINT will appear on the display screen. Other options allow key functions to be listed as in the third example. If you receive an error message, you may have specified an out-of-range key number.

Typical syntax:

```
KEY 3, "PRINT"
KEY 6, A$
KEY LIST
```

KILL

Type of keyword: Command, Statement

KILL is a disk BASIC command that deletes a file from the disk or I/O directory. A killed file will usually be overwritten with the next new file saved. If KILL returns an error, you may have specified a nonexistent file, incorrect drive, or incorrect file extension. Some systems have file locks and priority access. A locked file or incorrect priority user will usually generate an error message when trying to kill the file.

Typical syntax:

```
KILL "FILENAME/EXT"
```

See also DELETE, DESTROY, ERA.

L

LAND

Type of keyword: Operator

LAND is a logical AND function that operates on binary values. In the example below, the variable L will contain the results of a logical AND operation comparing variables X and Y. If LAND returns an error, you may have specified an incorrect variable type.

Typical syntax:

```
L = LAND (X, Y)
```

See also AND.

LEFT$

Type of keyword: Function

LEFT$ extracts the leftmost number of characters specified from the indicated string. The specified string can be a constant or a variable, as can the number. In most systems, the number can be specified as an arithmetic operation. In the first example, A$ is assigned the value "JOHN". In the second example, the first eight characters of L$ are printed. If LEFT$ returns an error, you may have specified a nonexistent string, or the number chosen may be out of range.

Typical syntax:

```
A$ = LEFT$ ("JOHNSON", 4)
PRINT LEFT$ (L$, 8)
B$ = LEFT$ (L$, 3 + X)
```

See also SEG$, MID$, RIGHT$.

LEN

Type of keyword: Function

The LEN command returns the number of characters in the string specified in the argument. In the example below, L contains the number 5. All valid ASCII characters are counted, including spaces and control codes. Most BASICs allow string concatenation in the argument, as shown in the third example. If LEN returns an error, you may have specified a nonexistent string.

Typical syntax:

```
L = LEN ("HELLO")
L = LEN (H$)
L = LEN ("HI" + A$)
```

LET

Type of keyword: Command, Statement

ANSI

The LET command is used to assign numbers or strings to variables. The variable on the left side of the equals sign is made equal to the constants or variables on the right side of the line. On most computers, the keyword LET is optional. In other words, A = 15 would be acceptable. Some computers don't allow the word LET and will only accept variable assignments as stated above. If an error message is returned, you may have specified a string variable for a numeric variable designation, or vice versa.

Typical syntax:

```
LET A = 100
LET A = 50 * 83
LET A = C + 25
LET A$ = "HELLO"
LET B$ = "555 - 2325"
LET X$ = C$ + A$
```

LINE

Type of keyword: Command, Statement

LINE is used to set the line length of input and output statements. The syntax requires a device number (zero is the screen, and the number may be omitted). In the first example, the printer, device number 3, is 132 characters per line, and BASIC will print 132 characters to that device before issuing a line feed and carriage return. Both device number and line length may be any numeric constant or variable. If LINE returns an error, you may have specified an out-of-range device number or line length.

Typical syntax:

```
LINE #3, 132
LINE #X, 80
```

LINE coordinates

Type of keyword: Command, Statement

The LINE command draws a line between the specified coordinates. The coordinates may be constants or variables, and usually math operations are allowed within the argument. Different options are allowed. In TRS–80 Extended Color

BASIC, PSET following the coordinates draws the line using the foreground color. PRESET draws the line using background color. IBM and TRS–80 use other options as well; a ,B (box) draws the line as a rectangle, while a ,BF draws the box and fills it with color. Epson computers use a color code to set the color of the line. If an error message is returned, you may have specified out-of-range coordinates or incorrect options.

Typical syntax:

```
LINE (100, 25)-(25, 30), PSET
LINE (10, 10) - (50, 50), PRESET
LINE (A, B) - (C, D), PSET, B
LINE (100, A) - (20, X), PSET, BF
LINE (X, Y) - (X + 10, Y + Z), BF
```

See also DRAW str, DRAWTO, GLINE, HLIN, MDRAW, RDRAW, VLIN.

LINE INPUT

Type of keyword: Statement

The LINE INPUT command is similar in most respects to INPUT. The major difference is that LINE INPUT accepts all characters from the keyboard except the ENTER key. LINE INPUT # is used to specify a buffer other than the keyboard. Commas, quotation marks, and other delimiters are accepted into the string. See INPUT and INPUT # for more details.

Typical syntax:

```
LINE INPUT L$
LINE INPUT "PROMPT"; L$
LINE INPUT #1, A$
```

See also INPUT, INPUT #.

LINE INPUT #
See LINE INPUT.

LIST

Type of keyword: Command, Statement

LIST will display the program in memory to the device specified (monitor, printer, and so on), usually the monitor. The two most common displays are continuous and paged. A continuous display will continue to list the program until it has been displayed. To stop a continuous list, a special key or key combination is entered. A SHIFT @, CONTROL C, or CONTROL S will stop the listing on many machines. A paged list will display one screen of listing and then wait for you to press a key. Most BASICs provide for partial listings by adding line number specifiers to the command. LIST 100–150 or LIST 100, 150 lists those lines between 100 and 150 inclusive. LIST 100– or LIST 100, will list from line 100 to the end of the program. In the last option, LIST –100 or LIST ,100 will list program lines from the beginning up to line 100.

Typical syntax:

```
LIST
LIST 25-50
LIST -25
LIST 100, 120
LIST 140,
```

See also LLIST.

LLIST

Type of keyword: Command, Statement

LLIST is a variation of the list command used by Microsoft. LLIST specifies listing a program to the printer rather than the monitor. All of the list options specified under LIST are allowed when using LLIST. LLIST usually does not return an error message.

Typical syntax:

```
LLIST
LLIST 100-150
```

See also LIST.

LN

Type of keyword: Function

LN returns the natural logarithm of the number specified in the argument. The argument may be a constant or a variable, and usually math operations are allowed within the argument. In the example below, L will contain the natural log of the variable X. If LN returns an error, you may have specified an out-of-range number in the argument.

Typical syntax:

```
L = LN (X)
```

See also LOG, LOG10.

LNOT

Type of keyword: Operator

LNOT is a logical NOT function that operates on binary values. In the example below, the variable L will contain the results of a logical NOT operation comparing variables X and Y. If LNOT returns an error, you may have specified an incorrect variable type.

Typical syntax:

```
L = LNOT (X, Y)
```

See also NOT.

LOAD

Type of keyword: Command, Statement

LOAD is a disk BASIC command that transfers a program from disk to memory. LOAD must specify the program name as in the example below. The program name can be a constant or a string variable. In some systems, the filename must be surrounded by quotation marks; in others it is not required. Some systems require an extension; others do not. Different systems have different maximum filename lengths, and certain symbols are not allowed as filename characters. If LOAD returns an error, there can be many different problems. The filename may not exist on the specified disk, an incorrect length filename may have been specified, or a wrong filetype may be being accessed. Normally, ASCII files cannot be loaded unless they are ASCII files of BASIC programs. Priority access systems may not authorize loading of the program specified if the user does not have the proper access code. An error or flaw in the disk itself will generate an error. Some systems have a RUN option that allows a program to auto-execute upon loading, as in the third example. Some tape systems also use LOAD. Commodore uses LOAD with a buffer number option rather than a filename. Buffer number 1, as in the fourth example, is the tape buffer. Buffer number 8 is the disk buffer.

Typical syntax:

```
LOAD "FILENAME/EXT"
LOAD THIS IS A FILE
LOAD "FILENAME/EXT", R
LOAD #1
```

See also BLOAD, CLOAD, CLOADM, LOADM.

LOADM

Type of keyword: Command, Statement

LOADM is a disk BASIC command that will load a binary file specified. An option that some systems have is LOADM "filename", offset (see the second example), where offset is a decimal number specifying the number of bytes above which loading would take place. The binary file has a start, end, and execute address stored when it is saved. (*See* SAVEM.) By using the offset, the computer adds the offset to the load and execute addresses and uses those numbers to transfer the file to memory. If LOADM returns an error, you may have specified an incorrect filename or improper filetype. BASIC programs and ASCII files cannot be loaded using LOADM.

Typical syntax:

```
LOADM "FILENAME/EXT"
LOADM "FILENAME/EXT", 1500
```

See also BLOAD, BRUN, CLOAD, CLOADM, LOAD.

LOC

Type of keyword: Function

LOC is a disk BASIC function that returns the current record number of a random access disk file. The buffer number specified must be a valid buffer number of an open file and can be a variable or a constant. In the example below, L will contain the current record number. If LOC returns an error, you may have specified an incorrect or out-of-range buffer number, or the file specified is not open.

Typical syntax:

```
L = LOC (1)
```

LOCATE

Type of keyword: Statement

LOCATE positions the cursor to the specified screen location. Syntax for the statement is LOCATE row, column, cursor condition. In the first example below, the cursor is positioned in row 1, column 1. The second example sets the cursor to row 10, column 10, and turns the cursor on. A zero in the cursor position turns the cursor off. PRINT statements following the LOCATE statement begin at the new location. If LOCATE returns an error, you may have specified an out-of-range row or column number. LOCATES is an option that can be used on the Epson computers to relocate the screen to a new position in the large virtual screen.

Typical syntax:

```
LOCATE 1, 1
LOCATE 10, 10, 1
```

See also CALL HCHAR, CALL VCHAR, CSRLIN, HTAB, POS, POSITION, PRINT@, VTAB, WINDOW.

LOCATES
See LOCATE.

LOCK filename

Type of keyword: Command

LOCK is a disk BASIC command used to remove access to a file. The file can then only be loaded and read. It cannot, however, be written to. Use UNLOCK to restore access to the file. The second example shows volume, slot, and drive number options. If an error message is returned, you may have specified an incorrect or nonexistent filename or option.

Typical syntax:

```
LOCK HELLO
LOCK PROGRAM, 1, 6, 2
```

LOF

Type of keyword: Function

LOF is a disk BASIC function that returns the highest record number of a random access disk file. The buffer number specified must be a valid buffer number of an open file and can be a variable or a constant. In the example below, L will contain the last record number in the file. On some machines, LOF will return the total number of bytes in the file. If LOF returns an error, you may have specified an incorrect or out-of-range buffer number, or the file specified is not open.

Typical syntax:

```
L = LOF (1)
```

See also EOF.

LOG

Type of keyword: Function

ANSI

LOG returns the natural logarithm of the number specified in the argument. The argument may be a constant or a variable, and usually math operations are allowed within the argument. In the example below, L will contain the natural log of the variable X. If LOG returns an error, you may have specified an out-of-range number in the argument.

Typical syntax:

```
L = LOG (X)
```

See also LN, LOG10.

LOGIN

Type of keyword: Command

LOGIN is used on the Epson HX–20 to select another program that resides in memory. There are five areas of memory that can be reserved for storage areas. In the example below, the computer will LOGIN to area number 3. If LOGIN returns an error, you may have specified an out-of-range number.

Typical syntax:

```
LOGIN 3
```

LOG10

Type of keyword: Function

LOG10 returns the base logarithm of the number specified in the argument. The argument may be a constant or a variable, and usually math operations are allowed within the argument. In the example below, L will contain the base 10 log of the variable X. If LOG10 returns an error, you may have specified an out-of-range number in the argument.

Typical syntax:

```
L = LOG10 (X)
```

See also.LN, LOG.

LOMEM:

Type of keyword: Command, Statement

LOMEM: is used to set the lowest point in which a BASIC program can reside. In the example below, LOMEM is set to location 2080. If LOMEM returns an error, you may have specified a number that is too low or too high for the machine memory requirements.

Typical syntax:

```
LOMEM: 2080
```

LOOP

Type of keyword: Statement

LOOP is used in conjunction with ENDLOOP to set up a loop that allows testing within any part of the loop. ENDEXIT and EXITIF provide the test structure. The example below demonstrates how the loop structure is set up. If LOOP returns an error, you may not have specified a loop termination.

Typical syntax:

```
INPUT X
LOOP
EXITIF X < 0
PRINT "X IS LESS THAN ZERO"
ENDEXIT
PRINT "X IS GREATER THAN OR EQUAL TO ZERO"
X = X-1
ENDLOOP
```

LOR

Type of keyword: Operator

LOR is a logical OR function that operates on binary values. In the example below, the variable L will contain the results of a logical OR operation comparing variables X and Y. If LOR returns an error, you may have specified an incorrect variable type.

Typical syntax:

```
L = LOR {X, Y}
```

See also OR.

LPOS

Type of keyword: Function

LPOS function returns the position of the print head. LPOS can be used to determine just exactly when a line feed and carriage return should be sent. In the first example, X will contain the current print head position. Y is a dummy argument. In the second example, a carriage return is sent if the position of the print head is greater than 64 characters from the left margin. In most cases, LPOS is not the physical location of the print head. The function is calculated from within the computer. Normally, LPOS will not return an error message.

Typical syntax:

```
X = LPOS (Y)
IF LPOS (Y)>64 THEN LPRINT CHR$ (13)
```

See also POS.

LPRINT

Type of keyword: Command, Statement

LPRINT has most of the same options and characteristics as PRINT and PRINT USING. The output of LPRINT, however, is to the line printer rather than to the display screen. In the example below, the word "HELLO" will be printed on the printer connected to the computer. Normally, LPRINT will not return an error message; however, if the printer is not connected or turned on, the computer may stop processing and wait for the printer to be connected and powered up. If the printer is unavailable, you may have to reset the computer or shut it off to regain control. Many computers allow an LPRINT USING statement as well. See PRINT USING for a more detailed description.

Typical syntax:

```
LPRINT "HELLO"
```

See also PRINT, PRINT USING.

LPRINT USING
See LPRINT.

LSET

Type of keyword: Statement

LSET is a disk BASIC command that left-justifies data in a file buffer. LSET is used with random access files to assure compliance with data fields. LSET must be used with a field command to place the data in the appropriate field. In the first example below, N$ has been fielded (*see* FIELD) to 25 characters. The name "JOHNSON" is put into the field with the J in the leftmost byte of the field. Spaces are added to the field to "pad" the string to 25 characters. The data (in this case, a name) can be a constant or a variable. If the name were longer than 25 characters, the information would be truncated, leaving only the first 25 characters in the data field. If LSET returns an error, you may have specified an incorrect buffer number.

Typical syntax:

```
LSET N$ = "JOHNSON"
LSET N$ = L$
```

See also RSET.

LXOR

Type of keyword: Operator

LXOR is a logical exclusive OR function that operates on binary values. In the example below, the variable L will contain the results of a logical exclusive OR operation comparing variables X and Y. If LXOR returns an error, you may have specified an incorrect variable type.

Typical syntax:

```
L = LXOR (X, Y)
```

See also XOR.

M

MAXFILES

Type of keyword: Command, Statement

The MAXFILES command is a disk BASIC command that reserves buffer memory space. In many systems, the number of simultaneous files available upon power up is three. If you want to reserve more or less files, thus expanding or contracting memory buffer space, issue the MAXFILES command. In the example below, three files are opened and buffer space is reserved reserved. If MAXFILES returns an error, you may have specified a total number of files that is out of range of the system, or you may have tried to reserve more file space than you have memory for.

Typical syntax:

```
MAXFILES 3
```

See also FILES.

MDRAW

Type of keyword: Statement

MDRAW is used to draw multiple lines on the graphics screen. The draw starts at current cursor position and connects points stored in the horizontal and vertical coordinate arrays. In the first example, the computer will begin drawing from current cursor to the coordinates stored in arrays X and Y. It will draw from there to the coordinates in the next two array locations. This will continue for five lines. Upon completion, the cursor will rest at the end of the last draw execution. A pattern number is allowed, as shown in the second example. If MDRAW returns an error, you may have specified an out-of-range or illegal variable, or out-of-range numbers in cursor array storage locations.

Typical syntax:

```
MDRAW X, Y, 5
MDRAW H1, V1, 15, 2
```

See also DRAW, DRAW str, DRAWTO, LINE, MRDRAW, XDRAW.

MEM

Type of keyword: Function

MEM is a function command that returns the amount of free memory available. In the example below, L contains the amount of memory left for BASIC programs. Normally, MEM will not return an error message.

Typical syntax:

```
L = MEM
PRINT MEM
```

See also FRE, FREE.

MEMSET

Type of keyword: Command, Statement

MEMSET tells BASIC the highest or lowest available memory, depending upon your system, for you to use in a BASIC program. It is used to protect memory from changes by the BASIC interpreter and can be used in machine language routine storage or other purposes where extra memory is required for your routines. If MEMSET returns an error, you may have specified an out-of-range memory location, or you may be trying to set memory smaller than what is currently required. MEMSET must be an integer constant in the range of zero to 65535.

Typical syntax:

```
MEMSET 32767
MEMSET 30000
```

See also CLEAR, HIMEM:, LOMEM:.

MERGE

Type of keyword: Command, Statement

MERGE is a disk BASIC command that will load a program file into memory without erasing any existing file in memory. In most systems, line numbers that exist on the disk will take precedence over line numbers in memory, thus substituting the disk file lines with lines existing in memory. MERGE is a useful tool for subroutine libraries. The subroutines can be called and installed at desired times. MERGE can also overlay parts of a BASIC program that is too large to fit into memory, as a RUN option is allowed (second example). For example, a program may have a screen print and line print routine, both located at the same line numbers. Depending upon the user's needs, the program can merge either the screen or the line print routine as needed, thus eliminating the requirement of having both routines in memory at the same time. If MERGE returns an error, you may have specified a nonexistent file or incorrect filetype. Many MERGE utilities must have an ASCII file to merge, rather than a BASIC file.

Typical syntax:

```
MERGE "FILENAME/EXT"
MERGE "SCRNPRNT/SUB", R
```

See also APPEND, CHAIN.

MID$

Type of keyword: Function

To isolate a group of characters in a string, use the MID$ function. The arguments can be specified as variables or constants. MID$ ("EVERYTHING", 6, 5) returns the string "THING." MID$ ("EVERYTHING", 2, 4) returns the string "VERY." If the last number is omitted, some BASICs return the entire rightmost string, while others return only the single character in that specified location. Some computers use MID$ as a replacement function as well. For example, MID$ (X$, 4, 4) = Y$ replaces four characters, starting with position 4 with Y$. If MID$ returns an error, you may have specified a nonexistent string or numbers out of range.

Typical syntax:

```
L$ = MID$ ("JOHNSON", 5, 3)
L$ = MID$ (Y$, 3)
MID$ (A$, 3, 2) = C$
```

See also MID$, SEG$.

MID$=

Type of keyword: Statement

To replace a group of characters within a string, use the MID$= statement. The arguments can be specified as variables or constants. In the first example below, the string constant "TOWN HOUSE" will become "BOAT HOUSE". The second example demonstrates the syntax to replace the third and fourth characters of Y$ with the first two characters in X$. If X$

is shorter than two, the entire string will be used. The length of the original string is never changed. If MID$= returns an error, you may have specified a nonexistent string or numbers out of range.

Typical syntax:

```
MID$ ("TOWN HOUSE", 1, 4) = "BOAT"
MID$ (Y$, 3, 2) = X$
MID$ (A$, A, B) = C$
```

MKD$

Type of keyword: Function

MKD$ is a disk BASIC command that converts a double-precision number into a coded string. Random access disk files may not contain numbers. Numbers are stored as strings and are converted back to numbers by the CVD function. In the example below, the numeric variable L is converted to a coded string and placed in the disk buffer. If MKD$ returns an error, you may have specified a wrong variable type.

Typical syntax:

```
LSET F$ = MKD$ (L)
```

See also CVD, CVI, CVS, MKI$, MKN$, MKS$.

MKI$

Type of keyword: Function

Function MKI$ is a disk BASIC command that converts an integer into a coded string. Random access disk files may not contain numbers. Numbers are stored as strings and are converted back to numbers by the CVI function. In the example below, the numeric variable L is converted to a coded string and placed in the disk buffer. If MKI$ returns an error, you may have specified a wrong variable type.

Typical syntax:

```
LSET F$ = MKI$ (L)
```

See also CVD, CVI, CVS, MKD$, MKN$, MKS$.

MKN$

Type of keyword: Function

MKN$ is a disk BASIC function that converts a number to a coded string. It is used in random access files to reserve the correct number of bytes for any number required. The number can be a constant or a variable. Usually, the number is converted into a string and set into a disk buffer at the same time, as in the example below. You have to field the buffer to conform to the number of bytes in the code. There are many types of numbers that can be specified using this system. If MKN$ returns an error, you may not have specified a numeric variable or fielded the buffer to correct length.

Typical syntax:

```
LSET L$ = MKN$ (25)
LSET L$ = MKN$ (X)
```

See also CVD, CVI, CVN, CVS, MKD$, MKI$, MKS$.

MKS$

Type of keyword: Function

MKS$ is a disk BASIC command that converts a single-precision number into a coded string. Random access disk files may not contain numbers. Numbers are stored as strings and are converted back to numbers by the CVS function. In the example below, the numeric variable L is converted to a coded string and placed in the disk buffer. If MKS$ returns an error, you may have specified a wrong variable type.

Typical syntax:

```
LSET F$ = MKS$ (L)
```

See also CVD, CVI, CVS, MKD$, MKI$, MKN$.

MON

Type of keyword: Command

MON is a disk BASIC command used to monitor the input or output state of the disk operating system. Issuing the command MON with one of the options will display communications with the disk on the monitor. This is an aid in debugging. Three options are provided. C displays disk commands, I displays input from the disk, and O displays output to the disk. You must specify one option as in the first example. The second example shows syntax for more than one option. Options can be listed in any order. If MON returns an error message, you may have specified an incorrect option. In the Epson computers and some disk operating systems, MON is used to enter the machine language monitor, as shown in the last example.

Typical syntax:

```
MON C
MON I, C, O
MON
```

MOTOR

Type of keyword: Command, Statement

MOTOR is used when you desire to change the state of the motor power supply. On the Epson HX–20, MOTOR will turn on or off the cassette motor, changing its state to the opposite condition. The second and third examples demonstrate the only two choices for the TRS–80 Color Computer. All three options can be used on the Epson. Normally, MOTOR will not return an error.

Typical syntax:

```
MOTOR
MOTORON
MOTOROFF
```

MOVE

Type of keyword: Command, Statement

MOVE is used to reset the position of the graphics cursor to the cursor position specified in the arguments. The MOVE command can be used to position the cursor for subsequent DRAW or GPRINT statements. In the first example below, the cursor will be positioned at location (10, 20). If MOVE returns an error, you may have specified out-of-range coordinates.

Typical syntax:

```
MOVE 10, 20
MOVE A, B
```

See also RMOVE.

MRDRAW

Type of keyword: Statement

MRDRAW is used to draw multiple lines on the graphics screen. The draw starts at current cursor position and connects points stored in the horizontal and vertical coordinate arrays. In the first example, the computer will begin drawing from the current cursor to the new cursor position stored in the array. The numbers stored in the array are relative to the current cursor position, and each array location must contain a number relative to the last specified number. This will continue for five lines. Upon completion, the cursor will rest at the end of the last draw execution. A pattern number is allowed, as shown in the second example. If MRDRAW returns an error, you may have specified an out-of-range or illegal variable or out-of-range numbers in cursor array storage locations.

Typical syntax:

```
MRDRAW X, Y, 5
MRDRAW H1, V1, 15, 2
```

See also DRAW, DRAW str, DRAWTO, LINE, MDRAW, XDRAW.

N

NAME

Type of keyword: Command, Statement

NAME is a disk BASIC command that allows the user to rename a disk file. Depending upon the system, NAME has several syntax differences. Check your disk manual for the specific syntax of your system. If NAME returns an error, you may have specified a nonexistent file, or you may have specified a new name that already exists. TRS–80 Model III BASIC uses NAME to renumber a program in memory.

Typical syntax:

```
NAME FILENAME AS NEWFILE
NAME OLDFILE/EXT AS NEWFILE/EXT
```

See also RENAME.

NEW

Type of keyword: Command

NEW is used when you wish to remove completely a program and data from memory. Caution must be exercised to save any resident program to tape or disk before using NEW if you wish permanent storage. NEW will normally not return an error message.

Typical syntax:

```
NEW
```

See also CLEAR, SCR.

NEXT
See FOR–TO.

NOMON

Type of keyword: Command

NOMON is a disk BASIC command used to disable the monitoring of the input or output state of the disk operating system. Issuing the command NOMON with one of the options will cancel the display of communications with the disk. This is the opposite of the MON command. Three options are provided. C removes display of disk commands, I removes display of input from the disk, and O removes display of output to the disk. You must specify one option, as in the first example. The second example shows syntax for more than one option. Options can be listed in any order. If NOMON returns an error message, you may have specified an incorrect option.

Typical syntax:

```
NOMON C
NOMON I, C, O
```

NORMAL

Type of keyword: Command, Statement

NORMAL is used to return from the INVERSE state. White letters are printed on a dark background in the NORMAL mode. Usually, NORMAL will not return an error message.

Typical syntax:

```
NORMAL
```

NOT

Type of keyword: Operator

NOT is used in IF–THEN statements to provide a negative or opposite condition. In the example below, the computer tests for equal value of X and Y. If found, the computer will not follow the instructions after THEN but will continue with the next line. If X is not equal to Y, then the statement will be completed. Normally, NOT will not return an error message.

Typical syntax:

```
IF NOT {X = Y} THEN PRINT "X IS NOT EQUAL TO
Y"
```

See also LNOT.

NOTRACE

Type of keyword: Command, Statement

NOTRACE is used to turn off the line tracer. TRACE is used in program debugging. Normally, NOTRACE will not return an error message.

Typical syntax:

```
NOTRACE
```

See also TRACE, TROFF, UNTRACE.

NSAVE

Type of keyword: Command, Statement

NSAVE is used to open and save a program file on diskette. NSAVE will append three blank file blocks after the last of the data is written for future expansion. The syntax for this is shown in the first example. The second example demonstrates that the file block size can be specified after the filename. This command is needed, as the DOS does not have dynamic file size allocation. If NSAVE returns an error, you may have specified an already existing file, disk full error, or other I/O type of error.

Typical syntax:

```
NSAVE FILENAME
NSAVE PROGRAM, 20
```

See also SAVE.

NULL

Type of keyword: Command, Statement

NULL is used to set the number of nulls printed after each carriage return. This is used to allow the print head to get to the left margin without losing any data. A null is represented as ASCII value zero. In the example below, the computer will print 25 nulls before sending the next line. If NULL returns an error, you may have specified an out-of-range number.

Typical syntax:

```
NULL 25
```

NUM
See NUMBER.

NUMBER

Type of keyword: Command

NUMBER allows the computer to generate BASIC line numbers for you. In the first example, the program numbering routine will start at line 100 and increment by 10. The first digit specified in the second example is the startline; the last number is the increment. Alternatively, you may just enter NUM with the desired parameters. If NUMBER returns an error, you may have specified an out-of-range line number or increment.

Typical syntax:

```
NUMBER
NUMBER 10, 5
NUM 10, 10
```

See also AUTO.

O

OCT$

Type of keyword: Function

OCT$ is a function that prints a string that represents the octal value of the decimal argument. In the first example, X will contain the octal value of the decimal number 10. In the second example, the computer will print the octal value of variable Y. If OCT$ returns an error, you may have specified an improper variable type.

Typical syntax:

```
X = OCT$ (10)
PRINT OCT$ (Y)
```

OLD

Type of keyword: Command

OLD is used to copy a program from tape or disk into the computer memory area. If OLD returns an error message, you may have a defective disk or tape, or no data were found on the media.

Typical syntax:

```
OLD
```

See also BLOAD, CLOAD, CLOADM, LOAD, LOADM.

ON ERR GOTO

Type of keyword: Command, Statement

This command is used to error-trap programs. In the example below, should there be an error in the program, such as divide by zero, the program will branch to line 10000. This prevents the BASIC interpreter from returning to the command mode. The error can be corrected in the program and control returned to the operator without loss of the program or data. If ON ERR GOTO returns an error message, you may have specified a nonexistent or out-of-range line number.

Typical syntax:

```
ON ERR GOTO 10000
```

See also ERRSET, ON ERROR GOTO.

ON ERROR GOTO

Type of keyword: Statement

This command is used to error-trap programs. In the example below, should there be an error in the program, such as divide by zero, the program will branch to line 10000. This prevents BASIC from returning to the command mode. The error can be corrected in the program and control returned to the operator without loss of the program or data. The ON ERROR GOTO statement must be executed before the error occurs, or control will return to the command mode.

Typical syntax:

```
ON ERROR GOTO 10000
```

See also ERRSET, ON ERR GOTO

ON–GOSUB

Type of keyword: Statement

ON–GOSUB allows selection of a subroutine depending upon the state of a variable. In the example below, if L is 1, the subroutine starting at 1000 is executed; if L is 2, the subroutine at 2000 is executed; and so on. If L is zero, or L is greater than the specified options, no subroutine is called, and the program continues with the line following ON–GOSUB. In the second example, a string variable is used. The formula converts the letters A, B, and C to their ASCII equivalents and converts them to the numbers 1, 2, or 3. This allows a program menu to be selected using letters instead of numbers. Some computers allow a keyword to be placed between ON and GOSUB, as in the last example, which will cause a GOSUB to occur on reading a lightpen result. Other keywords include KEY, COM, and STRIG, which check the function keys, communications port, and joystick trigger, respectively. If an error message is returned, you may have specified a nonexistent line number. Also, some computers must have a choice for every value of variable. If the variable is out of range on these machines, program execution stops and an error message is printed.

Typical syntax:

```
ON L GOSUB 1000, 2000, 3000, 4000
ON ASC(L$)-64 GOSUB 1000, 2000, 3000
ON PEN GOSUB 100
```

See also ON–GOTO

ON–GOTO

Type of keyword: Statement

ON–GOTO allows selection of a specific line number depending upon the state of a variable. In the example below, if L is 1, program control is sent to line 1000; if L is 2, the program branches to line 2000; and so on. If L is zero or negative, or L is greater than the specified options, the program continues with the line following ON–GOTO. In the second example, a string variable is used. The formula converts the letters A, B, and C to their ASCII equivalents and converts them to the numbers 1, 2, or 3. This allows a program menu to be selected using letters instead of numbers. If an error message is returned, you may have specified a nonexistent line number. Also, some computers must have a choice for every value of variable. If the variable is out of range on these machines, program execution stops and an error message is printed.

Typical syntax:

```
ON L GOTO 1000, 2000, 3000, 4000
ON ASC (L$) - 64 GOTO 1000, 2000, 3000
```

See also ON–GOSUB.

OPEN

Type of keyword: Statement

OPEN is used in a program that uses external data files on tape or disk. There are many system-specific ways of using the OPEN command. Typically, before printing data into a file or inputting data from a file, the file must be opened. One typical example is shown below. In this case, a file named "DATA" is being opened for reading by the program. See appendix 5 for more information on types of data files. If an error message is returned, you may have specified an incorrect device number, mode, or filename. Another possibility is an already open error. This error occurs if the file specified has already been opened. It also occurs in some machines when you try to open more than one file at a time. Many cassette systems only allow a single file open at a time.

Typical syntax:

```
OPEN "I", 1, "DATA"
```

See also CLOSE, CREATE.

OPTION BASE

Type of keyword: Statement

OPTION BASE is used to set the minimum number allowed in an array to zero. Most BASIC interpreters default to this mode. Executing the second example will give the array L a minimum value of 1. Choosing the OPTION BASE will define that base for all arrays that are dimensioned in the program. If you receive an error message, you may have dimensioned an array before stating the base option, or you may have used a number other than zero or 1.

Typical syntax:

```
OPTION BASE 0
OPTION BASE 1 : DIM L (50)
```

See also BASE.

OR

Type of keyword: Operator

OR is used in IF–THEN statements to provide alternative choices. In the example below, if either X or Y is 7, the computer will finish the IF–THEN command; otherwise control will proceed to the next line. Normally, OR will not return an error message.

Typical syntax:

```
IF X = 7 OR Y = 7 THEN GOTO 1000
```

See also LOR.

OUT

Type of keyword: Command, Statement

OUT is used to send data to a computer output port. In the example below, the number 65 is being sent to port number 1. If OUT returns an error message, you may have specified an out-of-range or incorrect variable.

Typical syntax:

```
OUT 1, 65
```

P

PACK

Type of keyword: Command

PACK is used to compress a BASIC program, removing excess lines, spaces, nonexecutable statements, and so on. In the example below, the file TESTFILE will be packed. PACK will remove any remarks or blank spaces that may have been included for documentation purposes or readability. Be sure to keep an unpacked version of the program for editing purposes. If PACK returns an error, you may have specified an illegal or nonexistent filename.

Typical syntax:

```
PACK TESTFILE
```

PADDLE

Type of keyword: Function

This command is used to read the game paddle. The argument specifies one of the two paddles. In the example below, PADDLE returns a number between zero and 228 to the variable X. The number represents the position of paddle number zero. If PADDLE returns an error message, you may have specified an out-of-range number.

Typical syntax:

```
X = PADDLE (0)
```

See also CALL JOYST, JOYSTK, PDL, PTRIG.

PAINT

Type of keyword: Statement

PAINT is a graphics command that begins painting the screen at the specified coordinates. In the example below, after the coordinates are listed the color number and border color number. Painting will be done with the specified color number and will continue to the border of the specified color number. The arguments may be constant or variable, and usually math operations are allowed within them. If PAINT returns an error message, you may have specified an out-of-range number within the coordinates or incorrect color number.

Typical syntax:

```
PAINT (10, 10), 4, 2
PAINT (A, X), 3, 1
```

PARAM

Type of keyword: Statement

PARAM is used to describe to a called procedure the variables to be received from the calling procedure. Its use and syntax are like DIM with the exception that no variable space is reserved. In the example below, space is being reserved for the variables X and Y.

Typical syntax:

```
PARAM X (10), Y (10)
```

See also CHAIN, DIM.

PAUSE

Type of keyword: Statement

PAUSE is used to temporarily terminate operation of a procedure. This statement is used to enter the debug mode. CONT is used to resume program operation. Normally, PAUSE will not return an error message.

Typical syntax:

```
PAUSE
```

See also BREAK, CONT, CONTINUE, STOP, UNBREAK.

PCLEAR

Type of keyword: Command, Statement

PCLEAR is a graphics command used to reserve graphics pages. In the example below, PCLEAR will set aside four pages of memory. In the computers that use PCLEAR, a higher resolution display requires a larger number of pages. If PCLEAR returns an error, you may have selected a number that is out of range. Another possibility is that you may have tried to reserve more memory than the system has available.

Typical syntax:

```
PCLEAR 4
```

PCLS

Type of keyword: Command, Statement

PCLS is a graphics command that will clear or reset the graphics memory to the specified color number. The number is optional, and if it is not specified the screen will clear to the background color. If PCLS returns an error message, you may have specified a number that is out of range.

Typical syntax:

```
PCLS
PCLS 3
```

See also GCLS.

PCOPY

Type of keyword: Command, Statement

PCOPY is used to copy the contents of one graphics page to another. A form of animation can be created by having several background pages with the same data. The moving objects can be displayed on one page while they are being redrawn on another. If PCOPY returns an error, you may have specified a page number that is out of range. PCOPY is used on the Epson HX–20 to copy a program from one memory area to another. If PCOPY returns an error, you may have tried to PCOPY into a page with a program in it already. The second example demonstrates the syntax for PCOPY.

Typical syntax:

```
PCOPY 1 TO 5
PCOPY 1
```

PDL

Type of keyword: Command, Statement

This command is used to read the game paddle. The argument specifies one of the four paddles. In the example below, PDL returns a number between zero and 255 to the variable X. The number represents the position of paddle number 2. If PDL returns an error message, you may have specified an out-of-range number.

Typical syntax:

```
X = PDL (2)
```

See also CALL JOYST, JOYSTK, PADDLE, STICK.

PEEK

Type of keyword: Command, Statement

PEEK looks at a memory location and returns a number (usually decimal) that represents the hexadecimal digit stored in that location. In an eight-bit microcomputer, the number returned will be an integer between zero and 255. In the line example below, the variable L will contain the value of the number stored in the memory location upon completion of the statement. You can use the memory map of your computer to find the numeric values of various important locations. If PEEK returns an error, you may have used a negative number for memory location, or you may have specified a nonexistent location.

Typical syntax:

```
L = PEEK (38822)
```

See also EXAM, POKE.

PEN

Type of keyword: Command, Statement

PEN is used to test and act upon activity of the light pen. The first example turns on the light pen function, while the second example turns it off again. The last example demonstrates that the pen may be tested and output routed to another part of a BASIC program. If PEN returns an error, you may have specified an incorrect option.

Typical syntax:

```
PEN ON
PEN OFF
ON PEN GOSUB 1000
```

PI

Type of keyword: Function

PI will return the constant 3.14159265. In the first example below, the computer will output 3.14159265. In the second example, the computer will substitute the constant in the formula. Normally, PI will not return an error message.

Typical syntax:

```
PRINT PI
XL = 2 * PI * F * L
```

PIESLICE

Type of keyword: Statement

PIESLICE is a graphics statement used to draw an arc and terminating lines radiating toward the center of a circle. The pattern is actually a sector of a circle. The first example shows how to draw a pieslice with horizontal and vertical radii of 50 and 70. Angles of 90 and 180 degrees are drawn.

Typical syntax:

```
PIESLICE 50, 70, 90, 180
PIESLICE X, Y, A1, A2
```

See also CIRCLE, ELLIPSE.

PLAY

Type of keyword: Command, Statement

PLAY is an audio command that will play music of specified notes. The notes are stored in strings, which can be constant or variable. Options include octave, volume, length, tempo, pause, sharps, or flats. Other options include execution of substrings and numeric or note specifications. In the first example, the string A$ will be played. In the second example, a scale is played with a tempo of 3 in the second octave. If PLAY returns an error, you may have specified out-of-range data within the string or a nonexistent note. Notes range from A through G only.

Typical syntax:

```
PLAY L$
PLAY "T3; O2; A; B; C; D; E; F; G"
```

See also BEEP, CALL SOUND, SOUND.

PLOT

Type of keyword: Command, Statement

PLOT places dots and lines in low-resolution graphics modes. The color is specified from a previous COLOR statement. In the example, a dot is plotted at pixel (10, 12). If PLOT returns an error, you have probably specified coordinates that are out of range of the system.

Typical syntax:

```
PLOT 10, 12
```

See also SET, POINT, PSET.

PMODE

Type of keyword: Command, Statement

PMODE is a graphics command that sets resolution and page display number. Computers that use PMODE have several resolution modes and pages of graphics memory. In the example below, resolution 4, page 1, is selected. If PMODE returns an error, you may have specified an out-of-range number. Another possibility is an incompatibility with the number of pages available—for example, trying to use page 4 as start page, when only two pages have been reserved.

Typical syntax:

```
PMODE 4, 1
```

See also GR, HGR.

POINT

Type of keyword: Function

POINT tests a specified XY coordinate on the graphics screen. Normally, if the point is reset (background color), a zero is returned. If the point is set, a positive integer is returned. In color systems, the integer represents the color number of the point specified on the screen. In the example below, L will contain the value of screen location (100, 100). If an error message is returned, you may have specified an XY coordinate that is out of range. On the North Star computers, POINT is used to set a pixel on the display screen, and it sets the new pixel location to current cursor location.

Typical syntax:

```
L = POINT (100, 100)
```

See also CALL GCHAR, PPOINT, PSET, SCREEN, SCRN, SET.

POKE

Type of keyword: Command, Statement

POKE places the number specified into the memory location. Both the location and the number specified can be constants or variables. Math operations are also usually allowed. Some computers also allow numbers to be entered in hexadecimal format. In the example below, the number 100 will be placed in location 16384. If an error message is returned, you may have specified a nonexistent memory location or a number over 255.

Typical syntax:

```
POKE 16384, 100
```

See also FILL, PEEK.

POLYGON

Type of keyword: Statement

POLYGON is used to draw a multisided polygon whose coordinates are stored in two arrays. In the first example, a five-sided polygon is drawn from arrays H and V. In the second example, a six-sided figure is drawn using the pattern option. If POLYGON returns an error, you may have specified out-of-range coordinates, improper arrays, or out-of-range pattern number.

Typical syntax:

```
POLYGON H, V, 5
POLYGON A, B, 6, 10
```

POP

Type of keyword: Command, Statement

POP pulls the location of the last GOSUB off the stack. POP is used when your program flow must not return from its last GOSUB. If no other GOSUBs are called and a RETURN is encountered, the computer will then execute from the previous GOSUB. Normally, POP won't return an error, but errors can occur because of improper stack addresses if POP is not used with care.

Typical syntax:

```
POP
```

POS

Type of keyword: Function

POS will return the position number of the cursor or printhead. In the example below, POS will return the number 8. The computer will tab six positions, print the character, and move the cursor to the next available print location. If there were no semicolon after the character, POS would be zero in many cases, because a print statement usually also sends a carriage return. If POS returns an error, you may have specified a nonexistent device number.

Typical syntax:

```
PRINT TAB (6) "A"; : L = POS (0)
```

See also LPOS.

POS
See POSITION.

POSITION

Type of keyword: Command, Statement

POSITION is a disk BASIC command that places a file pointer at the beginning of the field specified in the argument. The field in the file is defined as a group of characters terminated by a carriage return. Once the position command is given, all access to the file starts at the position number. In the first example, the position is not specified. A default of zero is assumed. In the second example, position number causes the file to start reading from the hundredth character in the file. If POSITION was used before, the previous position is added to the current position, and access begins from there. The position number must be preceded by the letter R. On the Atari, POSITION is used to place the cursor at a given screen position. The syntax is shown in the last two examples, which will instruct the computer to move cursor position 15 spaces left and 6 lines down. POSITION may be abbreviated as POS. on the Atari. If an error message is returned, you may have specified an incorrect or nonexistent filename or out-of-range number.

Typical syntax:

```
POSITION HELLO
POSITION PROGRAM ,R100
POSITION 15, 6
POS. 15, 6
```

See also CALL HCHAR, CALL VCHAR, CSRLIN, HTAB, LOCATE, PRINT@, SEEK, VTAB.

POS str

Type of keyword: Function

POS performs a string search and returns a number that represents the position within the string being searched of the first character of the target string. If the number returned is zero, the target string was not found. In the first example, L will contain the value 5, the position of the target string within the search string. You may use a number to specify from which character you wish the search to start. In the second example, the search will not start until the fourth character of S$. If POS returns an error, you may have specified nonexistent strings or a number that is out of range.

Typical syntax:

```
L = POS ("JOHNSON", "SON")
PRINT POS (S$, T$, 4)
```

See also INSTR, LEFT$, MID$, RIGHT$, SUBSTR.

PPOINT

Type of keyword: Function

PPOINT is a graphics command that returns the color number of the specified coordinate. In the example below, L will contain the color number of the pixel at (100, 99). If PPOINT returns an error, you may have specified an out-of-range coordinate number.

Typical syntax:

```
L = PPOINT (100, 99)
```

See also POINT, SCREEN, SCRN.

PR #

Type of keyword: Command, Statement

Upon the execution of a PR # statement, output control will be transferred to the slot specified. In the example below, a printer interface is located in slot number 1. At this point, all output will be directed to the peripheral. If PR # returns an error, you may have specified a nonexistent or out-of-range slot.

Typical syntax:

```
PR #1
```

PRESET

Type of keyword: Command, Statement

PRESET resets the specified graphics pixel to background color. (Read the statement as *Point* RESET, not *PRE*SET.) In the example below, the coordinates will be returned to the pre-specified background color. If PRESET returns an error message, you may have specified coordinates that are out of range for the display size you are using.

Typical syntax:

```
PRESET (100, 99)
```

See also RESET, UNPLOT.

PRINT

Type of keyword: Command, Statement

ANSI

PRINT prints the message you specify on the display screen, printer or other device. Other devices include disk or cassette, or other peripheral equipment. Access to these devices uses various formats. PRINT #1, "HELLO" prints the message to disk buffer number 1. There are many variations of the PRINT command, including printing to a specific location on the screen (TAB) or printing with specified delimiters. A comma following a print statement causes the next print statement to print in the next comma field. A semicolon causes the statement to be printed without sending a line feed command to the device. Many computers allow an abbreviation for entering the word PRINT; variations include ?, P., and P. Normally, PRINT will not return an error, though some of its variations might. Look up those variations separately.

Typical syntax:

```
PRINT X
PRINT A$
PRINT "HELLO"
PRINT "HELLO"; N$
PRINT A, B, "DATA"
```

See also DISPLAY, GPRINT, LPRINT, PRINT@, PRINT USING.

PRINT AT
See PRINT@.

PRINT@

Type of keyword: Command, Statement

PRINT@ is used in Microsoft BASIC to print to a specific location on the display screen. The screen is divided into individual memory locations, usually 1024. In the example below, the string will be printed on the screen with the first character placed at screen position 496. If PRINT@ returns an error, you have probably specified an out-of-range screen location number. Some computers use PRINT AT in a similar format.

Typical syntax:

```
PRINT@ 496, "PRESS ANY KEY TO CONTINUE . . ."
PRINT AT 100, X, A$
```

See also CALL HCHAR, CALL VCHAR, CSRLIN, HTAB, LOCATE, POSITION, VTAB.

PRINT USING

Type of keyword: Command, Statement

PRINT USING is a versatile formatting command in BASIC. It has many options and variations, not all of which are available on all machines. In the first example, the variable L is printed to two decimal places. If the number is less than 100, leading zeros are suppressed. Zeros at the right of the decimal point are always printed. In the second example, A$ is defined, and the PRINT USING statement will print the variable L within the number field. A double dollar sign causes the dollar sign to float to the right for smaller amounts. In the last example, the first six characters of L$ are printed. Other options include + and −, which will sign numbers; ! prints the first character of a string; ∧ ∧ ∧ ∧ will print a number in exponential format; a /, will display a comma after every third number; and ** will fill leading spaces with asterisks. If PRINT USING returns an error, you may have specified incorrect field parameters in the print string. There are several options and characters that vary from one BASIC to another.

Typical syntax:

```
PRINT USING "###.##"; L
A$ = "BALANCE: $####.##" : PRINT USING A$; L
PRINT USING "%   %"; L$
```

See also LPRINT, PRINT.

PSET

Type of keyword: Command, Statement

PSET turns on the pixel at the coordinates specified. In the first example below, PSET lights the pixel at (100, 99). Color computers may specify a color number as in the second example. If PSET returns an error, you may have specified out-of-range coordinates or color number.

Typical syntax:

```
PSET (100, 99)
PSET (100, 99, 5)
```

See also PLOT, POINT, SET.

PSIZE

Type of keyword: Command, Statement

PSIZE can be used to determine the number of file blocks the file will need for disk storage. The command can be used when creating new files to determine how much file space will be taken from the disk. Normally, PSIZE will not return an error message.

Typical syntax:

```
PSIZE
```

PTRIG

Type of keyword: Function

PTRIG is used to test the status of the paddle trigger buttons on the Atari computers. In the example below, the variable L will contain either a zero or a one, depending upon the status of the trigger on paddle zero. If the trigger is being pressed, the value will be zero. An open trigger registers a one. If PTRIG returns an error, you may have specified an out-of-range paddle number.

Typical syntax:

```
L = PTRIG (0)
```

See also PADDLE, PDL, STRIG.

PUT (coordinates)–(coordinates)

Type of keyword: Command, Statement

PUT in this format is a graphic command. The powerful statement places a previously stored numeric array on the graphics screen. Various options allow logical operations on the data before it is stored. If PUT returns an error message, you may have specified out-of-range coordinates or incorrect variable or options.

Typical syntax:

```
PUT (100, 99) - (120, 110), L, PSET
```

See also GET.

PUT #

Type of keyword: Statement

PUT is a disk BASIC statement used to place data from the specified buffer into the specified record number. The command is used in random access file systems. The buffer and record numbers can be constant or variable. In the example below, data previously LSET or RSET into buffer number 1 are placed in record number 12. If PUT # returns an error, you may have specified an incorrect buffer number or out-of-range record number. In many cases, the record number need not be specified. If not, the data are put into the current record (see LOC). The Epson HX–20 uses PUT% in a similar format to store data in memory.

Typical syntax:

```
PUT #1, 12
```

See also DEFFIL, GET.

R

RAD

Type of keyword: Command, Statement

The RAD statement is used to set BASIC math functions such as SIN, ARC, ATN, and so on, to radian mode. This mode allows output of data to be in radian format. To return to degree format, use the command DEG. Normally, RAD does not return an error message.

Typical syntax:

```
RAD
```

See also DEG.

RAND

Type of keyword: Command, Statement

RAND is used to seed the random number generator. When a computer is initialized, it will always deliver the same random numbers in the same order if the number generator is not randomized. If an expression following the number is greater than 1, the sequence of random numbers will be the same each time the program is run. This can be used to create repeatable conditions. If RAND returns an error, you may have specified an out-of-range number.

Typical syntax:

```
RAND
RAND 1
```

See also RANDOMIZE, RND.

RANDOMIZE

Type of keyword: Command, Statement

RANDOMIZE is used to seed the random number generator. When a computer is initialized, it will always deliver the same random numbers in the same order if the number generator is not randomized. In some systems, an expression following the number is the seed and is usually an integer between −32768 and 32767.

Typical syntax:

```
RANDOMIZE
RANDOMIZE 50
```

See also RAND, RND.

RDRAW

Type of keyword: Statement

RDRAW is used to draw a line from the current cursor position to a new position relative to the old cursor location. In the first example, a line will be drawn from the current cursor location to a position 5 units to the left and 3 units down. The second example demonstrates the use of the pattern option. The draw units can be in numeric constants or variables. If RDRAW returns an error, you may have specified out-of-range coordinates or pattern number.

Typical syntax:

```
RDRAW -5, 3
RDRAW 10, 30, 80
```

See also DRAW str, DRAWTO, HLIN, LINE, MDRAW, VLIN.

READ

Type of keyword: Statement

ANSI

READ is used in conjunction with DATA to allow a program to access data to process. READ will assign the data, either string or numeric, to the variable specified. Several options are shown in the examples below. When a data item is read, a data pointer moves to the next item on the data list. On some systems, READ is a disk BASIC command that tells the disk operating system to read the file specified. This syntax is shown in the last two examples. Some systems use a buffer number, as in the last example. If an error message is returned, you may have tried to assign a string to a numeric variable. An out-of-data error occurs if a READ is encountered and the data pointer is past the last DATA item.

Typical syntax:

```
READ L
READ L$
READ A, B, C
READ A$, X, Y, Z
READ FILENAME
READ #1, A$
```

See also DATA, RESTORE.

RECALL

Type of keyword: Command, Statement

RECALL is used to read a numeric array from tape. In the example below, array AR is read into the computer memory. AR must be dimensioned before it is read in if it is greater than 10 columns. If RECALL returns an error, you may have incorrectly dimensioned an array, or there may be tape problems.

Typical syntax:

```
RECALL AR
```

RECTANGLE

Type of keyword: Statement

RECTANGLE is a graphics-oriented command used to draw a rectangle with one corner specified by the current cursor position and opposite corners specified in the argument. In the first example below, the rectangle is started at the current cursor position and drawn with the opposite corner at (100, 100). In the last example, an optional pattern number is specified. If RECTANGLE returns an error, you may have specified an out-of-range coordinate or improper pattern number.

Typical syntax:

```
RECTANGLE 100, 100
RECTANGLE A, B, 23
```

REM

Type of keyword: Statement

ANSI

REM is short for remark and is used to comment on or otherwise document a program. When the interpreter sees a REM statement, it and all characters following the REM are ignored. Code that is to be executed by a program must not follow a REM statement on a program line. Normally, REM will not return an error message. Some computers allow an apostrophe or asterisk to substitute for the REM.

Typical syntax:

```
10 REM PROGRAM NAME
20 ' DATE / AUTHOR
40 * PRINT ROUTINE
30 REM VARIABLES USED: ETC.
```

REN

Type of keyword: Command

REN is used to renumber a BASIC program. There are three options, as shown in the examples. The first example will renumber the program in memory, assigning 10 to the first line and incrementing the lines by 10. The second example demonstrates a start line option, and the program will be numbered starting at line 1000. The last example demonstrates the increment option. This program would be numbered starting at 200 and incrementing by values of 5. All GOTOs and GOSUBs are accounted for and changed. If REN returns an error, you may have specified an out-of-range or impossible option, or you may have referenced a GOTO or GOSUB to a nonexistent line.

Typical syntax:

```
REN
REN 1000
REN 200, 5
```

See also RENUM, RESEQUENCE.

RENAME

Type of keyword: Command, Statement

RENAME is a disk BASIC command that allows the user to rename a disk file. Depending upon the system, RENAME has several syntax differences. The examples below demonstrate two different syntax types. Check your disk manual for the specific syntax of your system. If RENAME returns an error, you may have specified a nonexistent file, or you may have specified a new name that already exists. Some systems do not check to see if a name does exist, and you may have multiple files of the same name—a distinct problem. BASIC 09 uses RENAME to rename a procedure in memory.

Typical syntax:

```
RENAME "FILENAME/EXT" TO "NEWNAME/EXT"
RENAME FILENAME, NEWNAME
```

See also NAME, TITLE.

RENUM

Type of keyword: Command

RENUM is used to renumber a BASIC program. Several options are allowed, including specification of the new line number, start line number, and increment. The first example will renumber the program in increments of 10. The second example does the same, but starts the listing with line 1000. The third example specifies that the first line will be 1000, renumbering from line 100 to end of program only. The increment is specified as 10. If RENUM returns an error, you may have specified an out-of-range or an impossible option, or you may have referenced a GOTO or GOSUB to a nonexistent line.

Typical syntax:

```
RENUM
RENUM 1000
RENUM 1000, 100, 10
```

See also REN, RESEQUENCE.

REPEAT–UNTIL

Type of keyword: Statement

The REPEAT–UNTIL construct is a loop structure that is used when it is desired that a loop execute at least once. The test is at the bottom of the loop. The example below demonstrates how the construct operates. When executed, the computer will print the value of X until X is less than or equal to zero. If REPEAT–UNTIL returns an error, you may have used one command without the other.

Typical syntax:

```
INPUT X
REPEAT
PRINT X
X = X - 1
UNTIL X < = 0
```

See also FOR–TO, WHILE–DO, WHILE–WEND.

RES
See RESEQUENCE.

RESEQUENCE

Type of keyword: Command

RESEQUENCE is used to renumber a BASIC program. There are three options, as shown in the examples. The first example will renumber the program in memory, assigning 100 to the first line and incrementing the lines by 10. The second example demonstrates a start line option, and the program will be numbered starting at line 1000. The third example demonstrates the increment option. This program would be numbered starting at 200 and incrementing by values of 5. RES can be used instead of entering RESEQUENCE with all options as shown in the last example. All GOTOs and GOSUBs are accounted for and changed. If RESEQUENCE returns an error, you may have specified an out-of-range or impossible option.

Typical syntax:

```
RESEQUENCE
RESEQUENCE 1000
RESEQUENCE 200, 5
RES, 10
```

See also REN, RENUM.

RESET

Type of keyword: Command

RESET is a disk BASIC command that closes any open files on a disk in any drive. RESET should be used whenever disks are being changed, and the disk file program was not exited by the program's normal end routine. Normally, RESET will not return an error message.

Typical syntax.

```
RESET
```

See also UNLOAD.

RESET coordinates

Type of keyword: Statement

RESET is a graphics command used to restore a specified XY coordinate to background color. In the example below, screen location (10, 10) is returned to background color. If RESET returns an error message, you may have specified out-of-range coordinates.

Typical syntax:

```
RESET (10, 10)
```

See also PRESET, UNPLOT.

RESTORE

Type of keyword: Statement

ANSI

RESTORE is used to return the computer DATA pointer to the beginning of the data list. Some variations include restoring only string or numeric variables and restoring the pointer to a specific line number. Another variation is using RESTORE to reset the disk pointer to beginning of data. Normally, RESTORE will not return an error message.

Typical syntax:

```
RESTORE
```

See also DATA, READ.

RESUME

Type of keyword: Statement

RESUME is used to return program control to a line in which an error occurs. Used in conjunction with ON ERROR GOTO, control will branch to an error routine when a BASIC error occurs. Upon program correction of the error, a RESUME command will return to the offending line. In many systems, RESUME followed by a line number (the second example) will cause control to return to that line. The third example demonstrates the NEXT option. After execution of RESUME NEXT, control will return to the line immediately following the line causing the error condition. If RESUME returns an error message, you may have a nonexistent or out-of-range line number. If the RESUME statement is issued before an error occurs, you may receive an error message.

Typical syntax:

```
RESUME
RESUME 1000
RESUME NEXT
```

RETURN

Type of keyword: Statement

ANSI

RETURN is used at the conclusion of a subroutine. Upon execution of the RETURN statement, program control is sent to the statement immediately following the GOSUB. The only error RETURN causes is a RETURN without GOSUB error. GOSUB stores the location where execution is to resume upon RETURN. If no GOSUB is given, the interpreter does not know where to return. On the North Star computers, RETURN followed by a variable is used to exit a defined multiline function. A syntax error is generated if the function RETURN option is mishandled.

Typical syntax:

```
RETURN
RETURN X
```

See also DEF FN, GOSUB.

RIGHT$

Type of keyword: Function

RIGHT$ returns the rightmost number of characters specified from the string specified. The string and number can be either variables or constants. In most systems, the number can be specified as an arithmetic operation. In the first example, A$ is assigned the value "SON". In the second example, the last eight characters of L$ arc printed. If RIGHT$ returns an error, you may have specified a nonexistent string, or the number chosen may be out of range.

Typical syntax:

```
A$ = RIGHT$ ("JOHNSON", 3)
PRINT RIGHT$ (L$, 8)
B$ = RIGHT$ (L$, X + 17)
```

See also LEFT$, MID$, SEG$.

RLINE

Type of keyword: Statement

RLINE is a graphics BASIC statement used to draw a line from one coordinate to another using relative cursor positioning. Its function is like that of GLINE, except cursor position is relative to the last cursor address rather than absolute addressing. Coordinates may be expressed in numeric constants or variables. In the example, a line is drawn from (10, 10) relative units from the last position of the cursor to (20, 20) units from the last cursor position. A pattern number is also allowed, as in the second example. If RLINE returns an error, you may have specified out-of-range coordinates or pattern number.

Typical syntax:

```
RLINE 10, 10, 20, 20
RLINE X1, Y1, X2, Y2, 100
```

See also GLINE.

RMOVE

Type of keyword: Statement

RMOVE is a graphics command used to move the cursor to a new position on the graphics display. Its operation is similar to the MOVE command, except that movement is relative to the last cursor position rather than absolute. Coordinates may be expressed in numeric constants or variables. In the example below, the cursor is moved 20 units to the right and 20 units over from the previous cursor position. If RMOVE returns an error, you may have specified out-of-range coordinates.

Typical syntax:

```
RMOVE 20, 20
```

See also MOVE.

RND

Type of keyword: Function

ANSI

RND is a pseudo-random number generator. There are several variations for the argument. In the first example, L will contain a decimal fraction between zero and 1. That is the most common usage. Another common option is shown in the second example. L will contain a random integer between 1 and 100. The argument will specify the upper limit of positive integer desired. If RND returns an error message, you have probably specified an improper or out-of-range argument.

Typical syntax:

```
L = RND (1)
L = RND (100)
```

See also RAND, RANDOMIZE.

ROT =

Type of keyword: Command, Statement

ROT will draw a shape from a previously defined shape table (*see* DRAW). ROT specifies the angle at which the shape is viewed. In the first example, the shape will be drawn as stored in the table. In the second example, the shape will be drawn oriented 90 degrees from the data in the shape table. The number specified can be from zero to 64. If ROT returns an error, you may have specified an incorrect array or out-of-range variable.

Typical syntax:

```
ROT = 0
ROT = 16
```

See also ROTATE.

ROTATE

Type of keyword: Statement

The ROTATE command is used to set the rotation angle in degrees for relative graphics displays. After issuing the ROTATE command, all relative graphics commands will be rotated the specified angle before being drawn. All relative commands are affected by the ROTATE command. In the example below, all relative commands will be executed 45 degrees from where they are specified. If ROTATE returns an error, you may have specified an illegal angle.

Typical syntax:

```
ROTATE 45
```

See also ROT.

RPOINT

Type of keyword: Statement

RPOINT is a graphics BASIC command used to set a pixel at a relative location from the current cursor location. The cursor position is updated to the current location. In the first example below, the cursor is moved 5 units right and 5 units down from the current cursor position. The second example demonstrates use of the pattern option. If RPOINT returns an error, you may have specified an out-of-range cursor location.

Typical syntax:

```
RPOINT 5, 5
RPOINT X, Y, 100
```

See also PLOT, POINT, PSET, SET.

RSET

Type of keyword: Statement

RSET is a disk BASIC command that right-justifies data in a file buffer. RSET is used with random access files to assure compliance with data fields. RSET must be used with a field command to place the data in the appropriate field. In the first example below, Z$ has been fielded (*see* FIELD) to 25 characters. The data "50801" is put into the field with the 1 in the rightmost byte of the field. Spaces are added to the beginning of the field to pad the data to 25 characters. The data (in this case a zip code) can be a constant or a variable. If the data were longer than 25 characters, the information would be truncated, leaving only the last 25 characters in the data field. If RSET returns an error, you may have specified an incorrect buffer number.

Typical syntax:

```
RSET Z$ = "50801"
RSET Z$ = L$
```

See also LSET.

RUN

Type of keyword: Command, Statement

RUN is used to begin execution of a program. In most interpreters, RUN also resets all variables to zero or null. In the second example, variables are reset, and program execution starts at line 175. In the third example, the program named "HELLO" will be loaded from the disk and executed. Note that some computers require quotation marks around the program name. If RUN returns an error, you may have specified a nonexistent line number or incorrect or improper filename.

Typical syntax:

```
RUN
RUN 175
RUN HELLO
```

See also BRUN, EXEC.

S

SAVE

Type of keyword: Command

SAVE creates a disk program file that can be accessed by using the LOAD command. A filename can be assigned using SAVE "filename". Other variations include SAVE "filename", A, which will save a program on tape using the ASCII format. BASIC words are not tokenized, allowing programs to be loaded into text editors and other utilities for modification, editing, and so on. An error message usually indicates that an improper filename or incorrect filename length has been specified.

Typical syntax:

```
SAVE FILENAME
SAVE "FILENAME/EXT"
SAVE "FILENAME", A
```

See also BSAVE, CSAVE, CSAVEM, NSAVE, SAVEM.

SAVEM

Type of keyword: Command, Statement

SAVEM creates a tape machine language file that can be accessed by using the LOADM command. A filename is specified, as are the start, end, and execute addresses. In the example below, the program "filename" is being saved. Start address is at memory location 16100, end address is at 16384, and program execution will begin at 16120. If an error message is returned, you may have specified an improper filename or nonexistent or out-of-range memory locations.

Typical syntax:

```
SAVEM "FILENAME", 16000, 16384, 16100
```

See also BSAVE, CSAVE, SAVE.

SCALE

Type of keyword: Command, Statement

SCALE will specify a size for a shape to be drawn using DRAW or XDRAW. SCALE can range from zero to 255. In the first example below, a SCALE of 1 is set. All DRAW commands will be 1:1. In the second example, a line drawn 1 unit long will be extended 255 units. On the North Star computers, SCALE is used to set the size relationship between the graphics screen and user data. The third example demonstrates this use. User numbers are displayed on the screen 10 units for each unit of horizontal and vertical on the graphics screen. If SCALE returns an error, you may have specified an out-of-range argument.

Typical syntax:

```
SCALE = 1
SCALE = 255
SCALE 10, 10
```

SCR

Type of keyword: Command

SCR is used to scratch a current program and its data in memory. Caution must be exercised to save any resident program to tape or disk before using SCR if you wish permanent storage. SCR will normally not return an error message.

Typical syntax:

```
SCR
```

See also CLEAR, NEW.

SCREEN

Type of keyword: Function

SCREEN is used to test a given screen position for a character or color. In the first example, X will contain the ASCII value of the character at coordinates (20, 20). In the second example, the variable L will contain the color of the character at location (5, 5). If SCREEN returns an error, you may have specified out-of-range coordinates.

Typical syntax:

```
L = SCREEN (20, 20)
L = SCREEN (5, 5, 1)
```

See also POINT, PPOINT, SCRN.

SCREEN number

Type of keyword: Command, Statement

SCREEN specifies a graphics or text screen display and a particular color set. If SCREEN returns an error, you may have specified an out-of-range parameter.

Typical syntax:

```
SCREEN 1, 1
```

See also COLOR, GOFF, GON, GR, HGR, TEXT.

SCRN

Type of keyword: Command, Statement

SCRN is used in the low-resolution graphics mode to identify the color of the pixel identified in the coordinates. In the example below, X will contain the color number value of the pixel located at (20, 20). If SCRN returns an error, you may have specified out-of-range coordinate values.

Typical syntax:

```
X = SCRN (20, 20)
```

See also GCHAR, POINT, PPOINT, SCREEN.

SCROLL

Type of keyword: Command, Statement

SCROLL is used on the Epson HX–20 to change the speed of display and to enable or disable horizontal scrolling. There are several options to SCROLL. The first example demonstrates setting scrolling speed to slow, while the second example enables horizontal scrolling. If SCROLL returns an error, you may have specified an out-of-range parameter or option. SCROLL is also used on the Timex/Sinclair computers to cause the screen display to move up one line. Any subsequent PRINT statement will be printed on the blank line created by the SCROLL statement.

Typical syntax:

```
SCROLL 0
SCROLL 9, 1
SCROLL
```

SEEK

Type of keyword: Statement

SEEK is a disk BASIC command that allows repositioning of the disk file pointer to the desired byte. This allows the program to locate individual fields or even characters within the file. In the first example, the data pointer is placed at the zero byte in the path numbered 1. The second example sets the data byte to 200 in file number 3. If SEEK returns an error, you may have specified an out-of-range path number or byte number.

Typical syntax:

```
SEEK #1, 0
SEEK #3, 200
```

See also POSITION.

SEG$

Type of keyword: Function

SEG$ can be used to isolate a group of characters within a string. You may specify the string and numbers as variables or constants. SEG$ ("EVERYTHING", 6, 5) returns the string "THING". If the last number is zero, the computer will return the null string. In the first example, L$ will contain "SON". In the second example, L$ will contain the first three characters of Y$. If SEG$ returns an error, you may have specified a nonexistent string or numbers out of range.

Typical syntax:

```
L$ = SEG$ ("JOHNSON", 5, 3)
L$ = SEG$ (Y$, 1, 3)
```

See also MID$.

SET

Type of keyword: Command, Statement

SET lights a specific screen location to its predefined color. Screen location is specified by XY coordinates. X and Y can be variables or constants, and math operations are usually allowed in the argument. In monochrome systems, SET lights the location. Variations on SET include specifying a color number, as in the second example, which sets the coordinates to color number 2. If an error message is returned, you may have specified an out-of-range coordinate or color number.

Typical syntax:

```
SET (10, 15)
SET (10, 10, 2)
```

See also PLOT, POINT, PSET.

SETCOLOR

Type of keyword: Command, Statement

SETCOLOR is used to change the background color and intensity on the Atari computers. In the example below, background is set to color register 4, color 12, and intensity 8. Either constants or variables may be used in the statement. If SETCOLOR returns an error, you may have specified an out-of-range number.

Typical syntax:

```
SETCOLOR 4, 12, 8
SETCOLOR R, C, L
```

See also CALL COLOR, COLOR.

SGN

Type of keyword: Function

SGN returns the sign of the argument specified. Normally, SGN will return a −1 if the number is negative, a zero if zero, and +1 if the number is positive. The argument can be a constant or a variable, and most machines allow math operations inside the argument. If SGN returns an error, the argument specified may be out of range of the interpreter.

Typical syntax:

```
L = SGN (9)
PRINT SGN (L)
Y = SGN (73 - 123 * 3/3)
```

SHELL

Type of keyword: Statement

SHELL is a BASIC statement used to call the disk operating system to provide some disk access to the BASIC program. SHELL must be followed by a string that contains the command to be executed. Upon execution of the command, BASIC is suspended until completion. When done, control returns to the BASIC program. If SHELL returns an error, you may have specified an incorrect command or improper or nonexistent string.

Typical syntax:

```
SHELL "COPY FILE1, FILE2"
SHELL "KILL TESTFILE"
```

SHLOAD

Type of keyword: Command, Statement

SHLOAD is used to load a previously defined shape table from the cassette tape. The shape table is stored in binary format, and HIMEM can be used to protect it from your BASIC program. Normally, SHLOAD will not return an error message. If there is a problem with the tape or file, only pressing RESET will restore control to the user.

Typical syntax:

```
SHLOAD
```

SIN

Type of keyword: Function

ANSI

The SIN function returns the sine of an angle expressed in radians. The argument can be either constant or variable format and can usually be a mathematic operation. If SIN returns an error, you may have specified an out-of-range argument.

Typical syntax:

```
X = SIN (90)
Y = SIN (L)
```

See also ACS, ARCSIN.

SKIPF

Type of keyword: Command

SKIPF is used on the TRS–80 Color Computer to read but not load a cassette file. SKIPF will test a file to verify a proper save. A filename may be specified, and the computer will bypass all files up to and including the file specified. If SKIPF returns an error message, the file being read may be defective, or the filename specified is incorrect.

Typical syntax:

```
SKIPF
SKIPF "PROGRAM"
```

See also CLOAD.

SLOW

Type of keyword: Command, Statement

SLOW is a system-specific command that puts a Timex/Sinclair computer into the normal speed mode. When placed in fast mode, the computer does not update the screen display so that maximum effort can be placed in operating on data. SLOW will return the computer to normal mode. Normally, SLOW will not return an error message.

Typical syntax:

```
SLOW
```

See also FAST.

SOUND

Type of keyword: Function

The SOUND command is used to generate audio tones in the TV speaker. In the first example, the first number specifies the duration of the tone, and the second number specifies its frequency. The argument can be expressed as a constant, variable, or math operation. The third example contains the syntax for the Atari computers. In the example, the command selects sound register number 2, pitch 200, distortion amount 10, and volume 15. If an error message is returned, you may have specified an out-of-range argument.

Typical syntax:

```
SOUND 100, 1
SOUND A, B
SOUND 2, 200, 10, 15
```

See also BEEP, CALL SOUND, PLAY.

SPACE$

Type of keyword: Function

SPACE$ is used within a PRINT statement to print a number of blank spaces. The number of spaces to be printed is stored in the argument. The range of the argument must be between zero and 255 inclusive. In the example below, the computer will print 50 spaces. If SPACE$ returns an error, you may have specified an argument that is out of range.

Typical syntax:

```
PRINT SPACE$ (50)
```

See also SPC, STRING$, TAB.

SPC

Type of keyword: Function

SPC is used within a PRINT statement to print a number of blank spaces. The number of spaces to be printed is stored in the argument. In most systems, the number of spaces can be between zero and 255. In the example below, 50 spaces will be printed on the monitor, starting at the current cursor position. If SPC returns an error, you may have specified an out-of-range variable.

Typical syntax:

```
PRINT SPC (50)
```

See also SPACE$, STRING$, TAB.

SPEED

Type of keyword: Command, Statement

SPEED is used to control the speed of output to the monitor or peripheral device. SPEED is fastest when set to 255 and slowest at zero. In the example below, SPEED is set to the value of variable X. If SPEED returns an error, you may have specified an out-of-range variable.

Typical syntax:

```
SPEED = X
```

SQ

Type of keyword: Function

SQ is a function that will return the square of a number. In the example below, X will contain the square of the number 15. If SQ returns an error, you may have specified an out-of-range number or variable.

Typical syntax:

```
X = SQ (15)
X = SQ (N)
```

SQR

Type of keyword: Function

ANSI

SQR returns the square root of the number specified in the argument. The argument can be a constant or a variable. In the example below, L will contain the square root of variable X. If SQR returns an error, you may have specified an out-of-range variable.

Typical syntax:

```
L = SQR (X)
```

See also SQRT.

SQRT

Type of keyword: Function

SQRT returns the square root of the number specified in the argument. The argument can be a constant or a variable. In the example below, L will contain the square root of variable X. If SQRT returns an error, you may have specified an out-of-range variable.

Typical syntax:

```
L = SQRT (X)
```

See also SQR.

STAT

Type of keyword: Command, Statement

STAT is used on the Epson HX–20 to check the status of the five program areas in the computer. There are several options, including obtaining status of the area presently in use, all areas, size of program in an area, and the titles of areas. If STAT returns an error, you may have specified an out-of-range area number.

Typical syntax:

```
STAT
STAT 4
STAT ALL
```

STEP
See FOR–TO.

STICK

Type of keyword: Function

STICK is used to read the position of the computer joystick port. In the example below, the computer will read joystick zero and return a number indicating its status in variable L. The port number can be either a constant or a variable. If STICK returns an error, you may have specified an out-of-range joystick number.

Typical syntax:

```
L = STICK (0)
```

See also CALL JOYST, JOYSTK, PADDLE, PDL.

STOP

Type of keyword: Statement

ANSI

STOP is used in a BASIC program to cease program execution. When inserted in a program line, the program will stop execution at that point. Usually, a BREAK IN line number message will be printed to indicate where execution ended. This statement is usually used during the debugging stage of programming. Program execution can be continued using the CONT statement. STOP will not usually return an error message. STOP is used in TI BASIC interchangeably with END.

Typical syntax:

```
STOP
```

See also BREAK, CONT, CONTINUE, PAUSE, UNBREAK.

STORE

Type of keyword: Command, Statement

The STORE command is used to save a numeric array on tape. RECALL is used to read the array back into memory. In the example below, the array X is output to a tape device. Normally, STORE will not return an error; however, data may be garbled, or an error message might occur if the array stored is not dimensioned exactly as the array being recalled. A recalled array does not have to have the same variable as a stored array.

Typical syntax:

```
STORE X
```

STR$

Type of keyword: Function

STR$ converts a numeric constant or variable to a string variable. Used in combination with VAL, math and string operations can be performed on all variables. In the example below, L$ will contain a string variable identical to the numeric variable in the argument. If STR$ returns an error, you may have specified a nonexistent number.

Typical syntax:

```
L$ = STR$ (L)
```

STRIG

Type of keyword: Function

STRIG is used to check the status of the fire button on the computer joystick. In the first example below, L will contain either a zero or a 1, depending upon whether or not the button on joystick zero is being pressed. If L contains a 1, it is not being pressed. A zero indicates that the trigger is closed. The second example shows a different syntax for STRIG. In this case, STRIG ON and STRIG OFF will toggle the computer into testing trigger status between execution of program lines. If STRIG returns an error, you may have specified an out-of-range number.

Typical syntax:

```
L = STRIG (0)
STRIG ON
STRIG OFF
```

See also PTRIG.

STRING$

Type of keyword: Function

STRING$ creates a string of a given number of the specified characters. The argument can contain constants or variables, and the string can be specified as its ASCII code value. In the first example, L$ will contain 10 asterisks. In the second example, 20 A's will be printed. If STRING$ returns an error, you may have specified too large a string or an out-of-range ASCII code number.

Typical syntax:

```
L$ = STRING$ (10, "*")
PRINT STRING$ (20, 65)
```

SUBSTR

Type of keyword: Command, Statement

SUBSTR is a statement that performs a string search. SUBSTR returns a number that represents the position within the search string of the target string. If the number is zero, the target string was not found within the string being searched. In the first example below, L will be equal to 5, the first letter of the target string. The argument may contain constants or variables. If SUBSTR returns an error, you may have specified nonexistent strings.

Typical syntax:

```
L = SUBSTR ("JOHNSON", "SON")
A = SUBSTR (A$, B$)
```

See also INSTR, LEFT$, MID$, POS str, RIGHT$.

SWAP

Type of keyword: Command, Statement

SWAP is used to exchange the values of two variables. Variables may only be swapped if they are of the same type. In the example below, the values of the variables X and Y are exchanged. In the second example, K$ and L$ are exchanged. If SWAP returns an error, you may have specified a variable that is out of range.

Typical syntax:

```
SWAP X, Y
SWAP K$, L$
```

SYS

Type of keyword: Command, Statement

SYS is used to transfer control from a BASIC program to a machine language routine. The argument is the memory location, in decimal, where the machine language routine begins. After the machine language routine is completed, a return from subroutine (RTS) command in machine language will restore control to the BASIC program. If SYS returns an error, you may have specified a number that is out of range.

Typical syntax:

```
SYS 0
SYS 65535
```

See also CALL, DEF USR, EXEC, USR.

SYSTEM

Type of keyword: Command

SYSTEM is used when you wish to exit the BASIC interpreter and return to the disk operating system. On most computers, SYSTEM will close all open files, clear memory, and return to the operating system. Programs and data must be saved before the command is executed or all data will be lost. Normally, SYSTEM will not return an error message.

Typical syntax:

```
SYSTEM
```

See also BYE.

T

TAB

Type of keyword: Function

ANSI ·

TAB is used in conjunction with the PRINT command to begin printing at the column number specified. The number can be specified as a constant or variable. In the example below, the printer or screen will tab over 10 spaces before printing the message.

Typical syntax:

```
PRINT TAB (10) "HELLO"
```

See also HTAB, SPACE$, SPC, VTAB.

TAN

Type of keyword: Function

ANSI

TAN returns the tangent of an angle measured in radians. The angle can be a constant or a variable and must be converted to radians. If TAN returns an error, you may have specified an out-of-range variable.

Typical syntax:

```
L = TAN {X}
```

See also ARCTAN, ATN.

TAPCNT

Type of keyword: Function

TAPCNT is used on the Epson HX–20 to determine the position of the tape in the recorder. The position of the tape when it is totally rewound is stored in TAPCNT as zero. The second example will allow setting of TAPCNT to a desired value. From that point, all TAPCNT calls will be relative to the new setting rather than absolute. Use WIND to set the recorder position to any TAPCNT desired. If TAPCNT returns an error, you may have specified an incorrect or improper variable.

Typical syntax:

```
PRINT TAPCNT
TAPCNT = 20
```

TEXT

Type of keyword: Command, Statement

TEXT restores the text screen to full display and allows textual information to be placed anywhere in the text window. Normally, TEXT will not return an error message.

Typical syntax:

```
TEXT
```

See also SCREEN.

THEN

See IF–THEN.

TIME$

Type of keyword: Function

TIME$ reads the value of a memory location that is keeping track of real time. In the example below, L$ contains the correct time upon execution. Normally, TIME$ will not return an error.

Typical syntax:

```
L$ = TIME$
```

See also TIME$ =, TIMER.

TIME$ =

Type of keyword: Command, Statement

TIME$ = is used to set the real time clock in the computer. In the example below, the clock is set to 2:00. If you receive an error message, you may have tried to use numeric values or out-of-range time values.

Typical syntax:

```
L$ = "02:00:00" : TIME$ = L$
```

See also TIME$, TIMER.

TIMER

Type of keyword: Function

TIMER reads the value of a memory location that is keeping track of elapsed time. In the example below, L contains the value of the timer upon execution. Normally, TIMER will not return an error.

Typical syntax:

```
L = TIMER
```

See also TIME$.

TITLE

Type of keyword: Command

TITLE is used on the Epson HX–20 to designate a filename for a program area. When the Epson HX–20 menu appears, the title for each program area will appear. A title can be assigned or removed by the syntax in the two examples below. If TITLE returns an error, you may have specified an out-of-range or incorrect variable.

Typical syntax:

```
TITLE "HELLO"
TITLE " "
```

TO

See FOR–TO.

TR

Type of keyword: Command, Statement

TRON will turn on the trace function, allowing you to follow the operation of a BASIC program as it is executing. TROFF will turn off the trace function. Line numbers are displayed, as the program executes a new line, when the trace function is on. Some systems will display the results of mathematic operations when trace is activated. Normally, TR will not return an error message.

Typical syntax:

```
TRON
TROFF
```

See also NOTRACE, TRACE, UNTRACE.

TRACE

Type of keyword: Command, Statement

TRACE will turn on the trace function, allowing you to follow the operation of a BASIC program as it is executing. Line numbers are displayed, as the program executes a new line, when the trace function is on. Normally, TRACE will not return an error message.

Typical syntax:

```
TRACE
```

See also NOTRACE, TR, UNTRACE.

TRIM$

Type of keyword: Function

The TRIM$ function will print a string with all trailing spaces removed.. Its major application would be in data files where variable length data are stored in constant length fields. Usually, spaces are added to the end of data strings to fill out the field. In the example below, the function will print only the leftmost characters up to but not including the first space character at the end of the field. If TRIM$ returns an error, you may have specified a nonexistent string or incorrect variable type.

Typical syntax:

```
PRINT TRIM$ (X$)
PRINT TRIM$ ("HELLO   ")
```

TRUE

Type of keyword: Function

TRUE is a function that will always return the equivalent of 1 when used. In the example below, X$ will contain the character string "TRUE". Normally, TRUE will not return an error message.

Typical syntax:

```
X$ = TRUE
```

See also FALSE.

TYP

Type of keyword: Function

TYP is used to determine the filetype of the next data item in an open disk file. The value is returned in a variable; it will be zero for end of file, 1 for string data, and 2 for numeric data. The file number is specified in the argument following. If TYP returns an error, you may have specified an out-of-range argument.

Typical syntax:

```
X = TYP {1}
```

U

UNBREAK

Type of keyword: Command, Statement

UNBREAK is used to remove breakpoints in a BASIC program on the T1 99/4 computer. If you specify a line number or list of numbers after UNBREAK, breakpoints will only be removed at the specified line(s). Normally, UNBREAK will not return an error message.

Typical syntax:

```
UNBREAK
UNBREAK 100
UNBREAK 10, 1000, 10000
```

See also BREAK, CONT, CONTINUE, PAUSE, STOP.

UNLOAD

Type of keyword: Command, Statement

UNLOAD is a disk BASIC command that closes any open files on a disk in the drive specified. If no drive number is specified, the default drive is used. UNLOAD should be used whenever disks are being changed, and the disk file program was not exited by the program's normal end routine. If UNLOAD returns an error, you have probably specified an out-of-range or nonexistent drive number.

Typical syntax:

```
UNLOAD
UNLOAD 1
```

UNLOCK

Type of keyword: Command

UNLOCK is a disk BASIC command used to restore access to a locked file. The locked file can only be loaded and read. It cannot, however, be written to. Use UNLOCK to restore access to the file. In the second example, volume, slot, and drive number options are shown. If an error message is returned, you may have specified an incorrect or nonexistent filename or option.

Typical syntax:

```
UNLOCK HELLO
UNLOCK PROGRAM, 1, 6, 2
```

UNPLOT

Type of keyword: Command, Statement

UNPLOT is a graphics command used to restore a specified XY coordinate to background color. Coordinates may be expressed as variables or constants. In the example below, screen location (10, 10) is returned to background color. If UNPLOT returns an error message, you may have specified out-of-range coordinates.

Typical syntax:

```
UNPLOT 10, 10
```

See also PRESET, RESET.

UNTIL
See REPEAT–UNTIL.

UNTRACE

Type of keyword: Command, Statement

UNTRACE will turn off the trace function, which allows you to follow the operation of a BASIC program as it is executing. Line numbers are displayed, as the program executes a new line, when the trace function is on. Normally, UNTRACE will not return an error message.

Typical syntax:

```
UNTRACE
```

See also NOTRACE, TR.

USR

Type of keyword: Function

The USR function allows transfer of BASIC data into machine language subroutines. The argument can usually be numeric or string, and any results are passed back to BASIC through an identified variable. In the first example, the number 6 is transferred to the machine language routine, and upon receipt of a machine language RTS (return from subroutine) command, the variable X will contain any argument being returned from the machine language routine. In some systems, a DEFUSR statement is required, which specifies the location in memory of the USR function. In the second example, the argument represents which routine is being called (number 4). Y contains the variable that the routine will pass back to BASIC. (*See* DEFUSR.) If USR returns an error, you may have specified a nonexistent routine or out-of-range argument.

Typical syntax:

```
X = USR (6)
Y = USR (4)
```

See also CALL SYS.

V

VAL

Type of keyword: Function

VAL returns a numeric from a string statement. In the first example, L is equal to the number 10. VAL usually returns the value of all digits up to the first nonnumeric character. This means that numbers following dashes or colons are not part of the number. An exception to this is the dash as the first character. Most BASICs interpret this to be a negative number. If VAL returns an error message, you may have specified a nonexistent string.

Typical syntax:

```
L = VAL ("10")
X = VAL (A$)
Y = VAL (MID$ (A$, 3, 2))
```

VARPTR

Type of keyword: Function

VARPTR (read variable pointer) returns the memory address of the specified number or string variable. VARPTR can be used to locate and modify BASIC variables from machine language routines. In the example below, L will contain the memory address of the start of X$. If VARPTR returns an error, you may have specified a nonexistent variable.

Typical syntax:

```
L = VARPTR (X$)
```

See also ADDR.

VERIFY

Type of keyword: Command, Statement

VERIFY is a file-oriented command that is used to check the integrity of a disk or tape file. Depending upon the system, VERIFY has syntax differences. With some systems, the command VERIFY ON turns on the verify function. SAVEs are checked for proper file data as the file is being written. VERIFY OFF turns off the verify mode. In other systems, the command VERIFY filename will read and verify the contents of a given file. In both cases, if the file verifies correctly, no message or prompt is given. If a file is stored incorrectly, however, an error message is printed indicating a checksum error in the file. An error message may be returned if a specified file does not exist.

Typical syntax:

```
VERIFY ON
VERIFY FILENAME
```

VIEWPORT

Type of keyword: Statement

The VIEWPORT command is used to set up the visible area of the graphics screen. In the example below, the viewport is set to the coordinates (0, 0) to (159, 119). In other words, the viewport is composed of a screen of 160 by 120 coordinates or pixels. If VIEWPORT returns an error, you may have specified out-of-range coordinates or made the minimum and maximum coordinates identical.

Typical syntax:

```
VIEWPORT 0, 159, 0, 129
```

VLIN

Type of keyword: Command, Statement

VLIN will draw a vertical line at the appropriate position specified. In the example below, a line will be drawn from pixel 20 to pixel 40 on column 30. On a coordinate system the line would be drawn from position (30, 20) to (30, 40). If VLIN returns an error, you may have specified a number that is out of range.

Typical syntax:

```
VLIN 20, 40 AT 30
```

See also DRAW str, DRAWTO, GLINE, HDRAW, HLIN, LINE, MDRAW.

VTAB

Type of keyword: Command, Statement

VTAB is used to position the cursor on a vertical line. In the example below, the next print will occur at line 10. If VTAB returns an error, you have probably specified a number that is out of range.

Typical syntax:

```
VTAB 10
```

See also CALL HCHAR, CALL VCHAR, CSRLIN, HTAB, LOCATE, POSITION, PRINT@.

W

WAIT

Type of keyword: Command, Statement

WAIT puts a conditional pause into a program. The first argument specifies a certain memory location. A bit compare is done between the second and third arguments. If a bit in the second argument is not a 1, it is ignored. If you are waiting for a 1 or zero in that bit, specify 1 or zero in the third argument. When that condition occurs, the program continues. In the example below, memory location 32000 is checked for the number zero. When all bits in the location are cleared, program execution continues. If WAIT returns an error message, you may have specified an out-of-range argument. In some systems, the memory location happens to be an input port.

Typical syntax:

```
WAIT 32000, 255, 0
```

See also PAUSE.

WHILE–DO

Type of keyword: Statement

WHILE–DO is a form of loop and is similar to the FOR–NEXT loop. A condition is checked for true, and, if so, the computer processes the statements within the loop. Upon encountering the DO statement, a test for the true condition is made. If the condition is false, control proceeds to the line following the ENDWHILE. In the example below, a message is printed when X is a 1. When X is any other number, the program ends. If you receive an error message, you may have left out a WHILE, DO, or ENDWHILE command.

Typical syntax:

```
10 INPUT X
20 WHILE X <> 1 DO
30 PRINT "X = 1"
40 X = X - 1
50 ENDWHILE
```

See also FOR–TO, LOOP, WHILE–WEND.

WHILE–WEND

Type of keyword: Statement

WHILE–WEND is a form of loop and is similar to the FOR–NEXT loop. A condition is checked for true, and, if so, the computer processes the statements within the loop. Upon encountering the WEND statement, a test for the true condition is again made. If the condition is false, control proceeds to the line following the WEND. In the example below, a message is printed each time X is a 1. When X is any other number, the program ends. If you receive an error message, you may have left out a WHILE or WEND command.

Typical syntax:

```
10 X = 1
20 WHILE X = 1
30 PRINT "X = 1"
40 INPUT A
```

```
50 IF A <> 1 THEN X = 0
60 WEND
```

See also FOR–TO, LOOP, WHILE–DO.

WIDTH

Type of keyword: Command, Statement

WIDTH is used to set the line width of the line printer. Many systems default to a printer width of 132 characters per line. If you have an 80-character-per-line printer, use WIDTH to set the line length to 80 as in the example below. If WIDTH returns an error, you may have specified an out-of-range number. On the Epson HX–20, WIDTH also sets the margin and height of the virtual screen. There are several options to the WIDTH command.

Typical syntax:

```
WIDTH 80
```

WIND

Type of keyword: Command, Statement

WIND is used on the Epson HX–20 to change the position of the tape in the microcassette recorder. The first example will send the tape to the beginning and reset TAPCNT to zero. To find a particular file on the tape, select the TAPCNT to near the desired file location on tape, as in the second example.

Typical syntax:

```
WIND
WIND 200
```

See also TAPCNT.

WINDOW

Type of keyword: Statement

The WINDOW command defines the range of visible units within the viewport. The window is compared to the graphics screen and reorganized to fit into the 160 by 120 graphics screen. The numbers specified can be constants or variables. These numbers are expressed in units that match your application.

Typical syntax:

```
WINDOW -100, 100, 50, 50
WINDOW X1, X2, Y1, Y2
```

See also LOCATE.

WRITE

Type of keyword: Statement

WRITE is a disk BASIC command that tells the disk operating system to write data to the disk. Different systems have different syntax. Some systems, notably Microsoft, use WRITE in a manner similar to PRINT #. The difference is that WRITE puts quotation marks around the string stored on disk, whereas PRINT does not. This simplifies disk inputs, because an INPUT will then gather all data between the quotes, ignoring the usual PRINT and INPUT delimiters. Another variation on WRITE is used as part of a file open command. In this case, WRITE tells the computer to output data to disk, rather than READ data from the disk. After a WRITE command, all PRINT statements are written to the diskfile specified, rather than to the screen. See your disk operating manual for possible error messages.

Typical syntax:

```
WRITE #1, A$
WRITE FILE, DATA
```

See also PRINT, READ.

X

XDRAW

Type of keyword: Command, Statement

XDRAW is used to draw an already defined shape table. When XDRAW is used, it draws the table in complement color. This allows a drawing to be erased without erasing the background color. XDRAW is used in high resolution. In the example below, shape number 6 is drawn using complements of the existing colors at each point in the drawing. If XDRAW returns an error, you may have specified out-of-range coordinates or shape table data.

Typical syntax:

```
XDRAW 6
```

See also DRAW.

XOR

Type of keyword: Operator

XOR (reads exclusive OR) is used in IF–THEN statements to provide alternative choices. In the example below, if either X or Y is 7, *but not both,* the computer will finish the IF–THEN command. The XOR operator will work like OR, except when both elements are true, in which case XOR returns a zero or fails to act upon the IF–THEN. Normally, OR will not return an error message.

Typical syntax:

```
IF X = 7 XOR Y = 7 THEN PRINT "EITHER X OR Y IS
7, NOT BOTH"
```

See also OR.

APPENDIX 1

Programming Tips and Techniques

Many people can write BASIC statements and can even write a passable program, but they are not really programmers. A well-written program is easy to operate, read, and modify. This section describes and explains professional programming techniques that will not only make your programs look professional but will also operate in a professional manner. In addition, if you plan to convert programs from other versions of BASIC to run on your computer, there are tips included in this appendix.

The first task of the programmer is to make his or her program do a specific job. To this end, there are techniques that improve the operation of the program as well as make it easier to read and modify. Remember that BASIC is a foreign language and, much like any foreign language, it must be cultivated. Skills are developed by usage, not by reading about them. The biggest mistake many programmers make is to sit down at the keyboard and begin coding (entering BASIC statements). In many cases, the method works, but, especially for long programs, the method is inefficient. Remember to be problem-oriented at first. Be sure to define completely the problem your program is trying to solve; it's easy to leave out small details at this point. You want to solve the problem in English before you attempt to translate the solution to BASIC.

The same mistake is often made by people who are converting programs. It is much more efficient to break the program being converted into its functions and to rewrite the program to take advantage of the power of your computer. Trying to recreate a program line by line will cause many problems in translation. Instead, look at the code with an eye toward breaking it down into functional blocks. Then try to recreate the operation of the blocks on your computer. Use flow charts and the pseudocode techniques described in this appendix to help you with the conversion.

Whether converting a program or writing a new one, analyze the steps involved in the solution and they will be easily separated. List these steps in order of execution. When you have broken the problem into short steps, each step or module can be written independently. Ideally, a module should be self-contained. In other words, if you were to give the module the correct variables, it should process and deliver the correct output even if none of the rest of the program existed. By constructing the program in this manner, a team of programmers can work on a problem, each separate from the others, and put their modules together to complete the entire program.

Single modules are thus easier to write than an entire program. Any changes often only involve a single module. Debugging can also be easier as problems can be isolated to a single module. Probably the biggest advantage of modular programming is the ability to keep modules as separate routines. These routines can be loaded into memory and renumbered to fit into a new program being written. Most BASICs have a MERGE function that will allow this. Even those that don't usually have a way of joining program modules via machine language routines designed for the purpose.

If you write programs in block fashion, always number in blocks of 1000. If you follow that convention and always use the same 1000 block, modules won't even have to be renumbered. For example, lines 1000 to 1999 will always contain code that loads tape files; lines 2000 to 2999 always write tape files; lines 3000 to 3999 always read disk files; lines 4000 to 4999 always write disk files; and lines 5000 to 6000 always contain print routines. When doing program conversions, try to keep intact any numbering scheme written by the original author. This can help tremendously in debugging the program. Use any module structure that the original author created.

The major constraint with the modular approach is that the data handled by the modules must be carefully defined in advance. This is because each module must work with the data and know exactly how the data are formatted.

One of the most useful tools of the programmer is flow charting. Each standard flow chart symbol has a function in the layout of a program. A simple program with flow chart is included in Figure 1–1. The oval indicates a program beginning or end. The rectangle indicates an instruction that the computer is to follow. Sometimes the rectangle is drawn as a parallelogram. A diamond box always has at least one entry and two exit points. The diamond signifies a conditional statement. In BASIC, this is the IF–THEN statement. A trapezoid indicates an I/O-oriented command. The hexagon-shaped box denotes a subroutine. Small circles indicate connectors in the flow chart, and arrows show the direction of program flow.

One of the advantages of the flow charting technique is that the programmer is forced to organize his or her program into functions. This organization process helps the programmer understand what each part of the program is to do and inevitably assists in writing it. Most flow charts will not include the actual statements, as in Figure 1–1. At the time you are doing the chart, you probably only have a hint about correct line numbers. One way programmers write BASIC in preliminary stages is to use pseudocode. Pseudocode uses BASIC-like statements that probably won't work on your computer. An example of the program shown in Figure 1–1 will make this clearer:

```
REM AGE PROGRAM
REM GET AGE
PRINT OPENING MESSAGE
PRINT AGE PROMPT
INPUT AGE
```

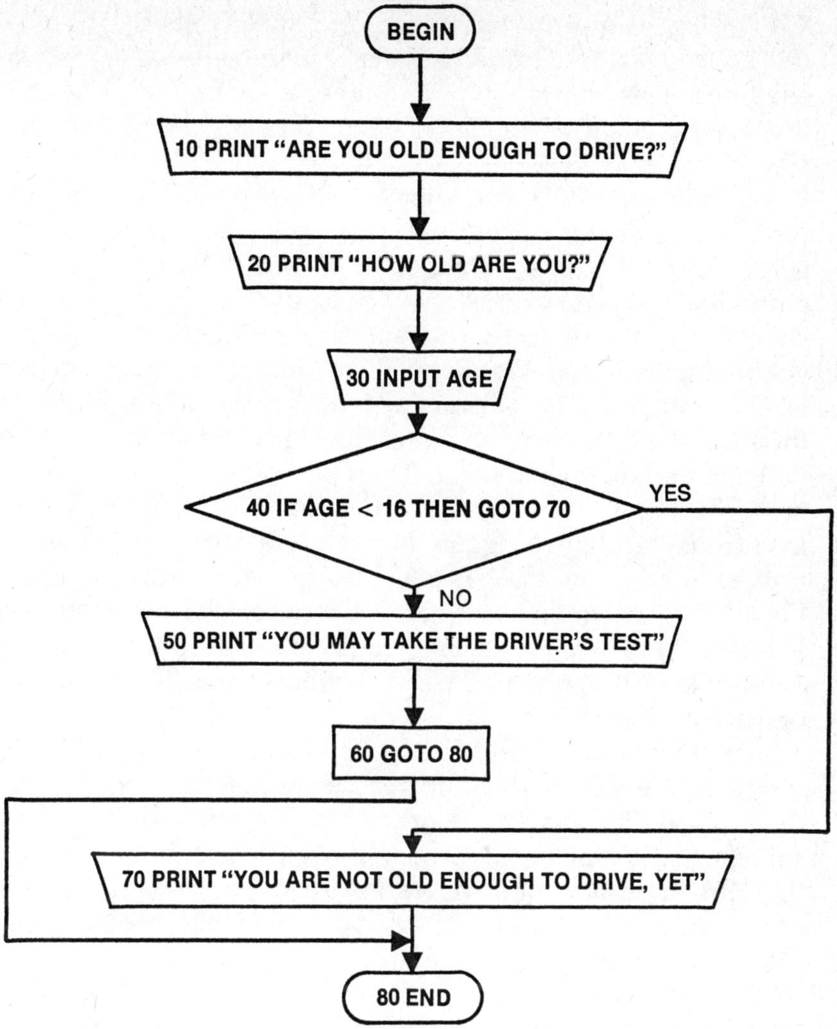

Figure 1–1

```
REM TEST AGE
IF AGE < 16 GOTO NOT OLD ENOUGH
PRINT ELIGIBLE MESSAGE
GOTO END
REM NOT OLD ENOUGH
PRINT NOT OLD ENOUGH
END
```

There are no line numbers, and statements like GOTO, GOSUB, and so on, only reference to remarks and module headings. This allows the programmer to be flexible in assigning line numbers when the program gets larger and modules start being assembled.

While we are on the subject of remarks, be sure to use plenty of remarks in writing your program. Even program authors forget, after a short period of time, how the logic of a particular program works. Any program of any importance should be stored in two versions: a running copy and a documentation copy. Documentation copies have their remarks left in, and program lines are spaced for easy reading. When the program is ready to be put into service, the remarks can be deleted and spaces removed. There are programmer's utilities available that will perform those functions on many machines. In addition, many program utilities will also pack lines. A packed line is one that has been assembled from many lines. The packing program inserts colons between all statements and keeps track of whether a line can be packed onto the end of another line. Program line packing probably saves more memory than deleting either REMS or spaces.

With removal of REMS and spaces and packing of lines, program execution speed increases. The BASIC interpreter doesn't have to waste time decoding REMs and disregarding statements or looking up unnecessary line numbers. Another hint: if you number your programs by 10, put remarks in lines ending in 5. It is an easy matter if you are manually editing the program to delete the lines ending in 5.

By writing programs in a top-to-bottom fashion and by constructing programs in modules, you will improve program execution and simplify the debugging process at the same time. Another helpful hint when documenting programs is to use remarks at the beginning of the program listing that identify all of the program variables. All of these hints will improve not only the operation of your programs but the ease of debugging them as well.

Programming Conversion Techniques

One of the most useful applications for this reference is as a tool for program conversions from one dialect of BASIC to another. This appendix will give you some insight into the kinds of problems you might run into and what steps you should take to accomplish the conversion. In addition, some conversions are nearly impossible to complete without a full understanding of the computers involved in the conversion. Other conversions might require hardware modifications to allow the program to work on your computer. In these cases, a decision must be made about how desirable the conversion is. We will take a look at how to tell if a program is not practical to be converted before you even sit down at the keyboard.

The first step in program conversion is understanding exactly how a program works. Try to choose well-written, well-documented programs to convert. It is difficult, if not impossible, to convert code written as in the example below:

```
1000X=10:AL=AL+ZD:IFZD>27ANDAL+17*23
=XTHENPRINT"NOTAPPLICABLE":GOTO50:
ELSEPRINT"TEXTOK":GOSUB1500:IFZD
=XTHEN2000
```

Can you imagine doing a program conversion on a 200-line program with most of the lines looking like that? You can't do anything about a program written that way, but you can make sure your programs don't look like that by following the examples outlined in appendix 1.

To understand the flow of a program, look carefully at the code and break it into functional blocks. If you have a flow chart, most of the work has already been done. If not, use the techniques in appendix 1 to create one, or use pseudocode if you prefer. Try to get several sample runs of the program and see the kind of output it generates. This will aid dramatically in formatting the output of your conversion.

If the program is graphics-oriented, use appendix 3 to assist you in understanding the general principles of graphics. In most cases, it is best to completely rewrite graphics routines to take advantage of the power of your particular computer. Again, sample runs are a requirement of graphics-oriented programs. Once you see the expected output, concentrate your efforts on duplicating the output rather than duplicating the code. The cross-reference guide in the dictionary can help by showing you similar graphics commands that you may find on your computer.

Sometimes screen displays are more easily created using a graphics editor. Most computers have editors available that create pictures that can be accessed by BASIC for use in your program. Animated programs are possible with many computers these days. If your computer has animated graphics capacity, you should use the techniques that work on your computer by analyzing the output of the program you are converting and rewriting them.

Programs that handle disk or tape files can be converted easily in most cases if you are familiar with the file-handling capacity of your computer. Use the techniques in appendix 4 to gain a basic understanding of how most computers handle files. Use those techniques and your BASIC manual to recreate the input and output of the program you are converting in syntax your computer understands.

One nearly impossible conversion is trying to make a random access disk file program work on a cassette-based system. Cassette systems have only sequential access. In many cases the conversion can be done, but only on a limited scale, as the random access routines must be rewritten to write and read the data in memory. If you have access to lots of memory in your system, you might make it work, but only at a limited capacity. Remember that the typical disk system can store more than 150,000 bytes, while you might only have 20,000 or so bytes available in memory.

Programs that use machine language subroutines may or may not be easy to convert. To work around these routines, you must know what they do and recreate them. Some machines use routines in machine language because their functions are not available in the machine that program was written for. You may already have that function built into BASIC. Machine language is often used for high-speed animation. Though these routines might be duplicated in BASIC, you would probably not be happy with their performance, as BASIC would slow their speed tremendously. Think twice about converting programs that contain high-speed animation techniques.

Programs that use PEEK or POKE commands provide their own set of problems. Usually, these commands are used when some particular hardware function is being accessed or when BASIC must be interfaced with machine language routines. Avoid program conversions involving a lot of these commands. In order to convert them, you must know the memory map of both machines in enough detail for you first to be able to figure out what a particular POKE or PEEK is doing, and, second, to transfer it to the equivalent location in your computer.

If there are only a couple of occasions where these commands are used, you might get by with discussing the purpose of each occurrence of the command with someone who owns a computer like the one needed to run the program you are converting. A good memory map of your own computer will in many cases show you the correct location of the PEEK or POKE in your machine. There may be occasions when the function cannot be duplicated.

One way to assist others in converting your programs is to avoid using these two commands as much as possible. If you must use them, then document, using REMs, the purpose of each PEEK and POKE in your programs. If this is done, the person doing the conversion will be able to determine what the command is doing, so that he or she may more easily devise a way to do the same thing on his or her machine. In some cases, the person may be able to omit the command, as his or her computer may have other ways of doing what you have to do on your machine.

Not every program can be written to work on every machine, but if you concentrate on programs that contain few exotic commands and break the program being converted into small, easily understandable blocks, you will improve your chances of a successful conversion. By following these techniques, you will find program conversion to be a useful and rewarding pastime.

APPENDIX 3

BASIC Graphics Techniques

Many computers on the market today have some powerful graphics techniques. BASIC has many graphics commands that can be implemented on computers ranging from liquid crystal display (LCD) readout portables to high-density, high-resolution multicolor systems. This appendix will describe some of the most commonly found BASIC graphics systems and will assist you in understanding graphics-oriented computer terminology.

Most graphics-oriented computers have different text modes and graphics modes. In order to use graphics commands, you must typically enter and use one of the graphics modes. Usually, this involves reserving extra memory for the graphics being stored, clearing the graphics screen, and calling up the graphics mode. Simple low-resolution graphics and string graphics (each to be described later) can sometimes be accomplished without the above steps.

Nearly all computer graphics displays are made up of small dots of picture elements. These elements are placed in patterns that create any desired picture. To see a graphic example of this technique, look at a newspaper photograph under a magnifying lens. Dark areas of the picture have large amounts of black dots spaced closely together, while light areas have few widely spaced black dots. Gray areas have larger quantities of black dots.

The same technique is used in computers. Each dot can be either set (lit) or reset (unlit). Light areas are represented by large amounts of dots that are set, while dark areas contain mostly reset dots. *Pixel* is the term most often used for describing individual dots.

Nearly all computers use set–reset graphics in one form or another, and they usually use a coordinate system to define the location of each pixel to be set or reset. The major difference between computers is in the exact syntax of setting or resetting a pixel and in identifying which pixel should be changed.

Most computers use a coordinate system to identify pixel locations. The screen will display a certain number of pixels across the horizontal screen line and a certain number of pixels in a vertical line. Using a hypothetical computer as an example, it might have 100 pixels across and 75 pixels down. The total number of pixels available would be 7500 (100 × 75). Using the coordinate system is easy. Typical syntax might be SET (0, 0) to light the pixel in the upper left-hand corner. Another commonly used keyword that does the same thing is PLOT. To light the second pixel in the first horizontal row, just SET (1, 0). To set the leftmost pixel in the second row, use SET (0, 1). To set the last pixel in the lower right corner in our hypothetical computer, use SET (100, 75). As you can see by this example, the first number is usually the horizontal pixel, and the vertical pixel is the latter.

The number of pixels on a screen determines the computer's resolution. The greater the number of pixels, the greater the resolution. High resolution demands more memory, as the computer must keep track of the status of a greater number of pixels. The advantage of high resolution is the ability to display pictures in greater detail. Some applications, such as computer-aided design, require very high resolution, usually greater than 100,000 pixels. Low-resolution graphics can be created with pixels as few as 22 across by 24 down. These large pixels are sometimes more appropriately called *blocks*. Block graphics can create identifiable drawings, though the pictures are very coarse-looking since the blocks make such large lines.

Block graphics can be created in many computers using set–reset techniques. In addition, some computers have block graphic characters stored in their memory as ASCII characters. Usually, this is possible because there are only 127 characters used in a typical computer ASCII table for the standard ASCII control codes, letters, and numbers. (See appendix 6.) Since most computers can handle numbers as large as 255 in a standard character format, this leaves 128 characters that can be defined as graphics blocks.

To access these characters, most computers use the CHR$ command, though a few allow characters to be entered directly from the keyboard. To see if your computer has character string graphics, use PRINT CHR$ (N), where N is a number greater than 127. If your computer has block graphics, you will see one of the blocks printed on the screen. Though the resolution of block graphics techniques is low, they have the advantage of being able to use the PRINT command to have the graphics displayed.

String graphics use strings of graphics characters that are oriented into special shapes. Figure 3–1 demonstrates this technique. In our hypothetical computer, ASCII values 190, 189, and 184 are used to generate three typical graphics blocks. The "dog" picture is created by putting the three character string values together into one string and printing the string. Animation can be achieved by clearing the screen and printing the blocks in successive locations using PRINT@ or a command of similar nature. More sophisticated techniques can be applied by printing black blocks or resetting the old pixels and then printing the characters at a new location.

Color graphics can be provided on many computers by using either block or pixel graphics. In a typical computer, color graphics require additional memory because the computer must keep track of the color of a given pixel in addition to tracking whether the pixel is on or off. Many graphics computers treat black as off rather than as a specific color value. Set and reset can be used in most systems with two major diffeerences. Some computers use the syntax as described for pixel graphics above but preface the SET command with a COLOR = command specifying which color to set the pixels. Some computers specify the color in the SET command, as in SET (0, 0, 1), where the 1 is a color number. In either case,

190 189 194

```
10 A$ = CHR$ (190) + CHR$ (189) + CHR$ (194)
20 PRINT A$
```

Figure 3–1

RESET is identical, as it resets the color to the background color. Remember, you may find other terms that use different keywords but do the same thing.

As was stated earlier, computers require that extra memory be reserved for graphics storage. Most computers reserve graphics memory in blocks that represent screens of picture information, which are often called *pages*. In some systems, one page is equivalent to one screen, though other systems classify a page as a certain number of bytes of memory, and a screen can be composed of one or more pages. In most computers, it is possible to switch back and forth between several pages of information, allowing more than one picture at a time to be stored in memory. A simple form of animation can be achieved by drawing a picture on the hidden page and displaying it while a new picture is being drawn on the other page. The technique works for simple animation and can be rather quick in action.

More sophisticated animation can be achieved by the use of GET and PUT if your computer has these graphics-oriented commands. GET will cause the computer to store a small rectangle of screen information into memory. PUT can then place the information anywhere on the graphics screen. An example might be drawing a car on the lower left corner of the screen, using GET to store the image of the car in memory, and using PUT to place the car into successive locations to the right. When done properly, the car will seem to move from the left to the right.

A similar capability is used in many computers with hardware that uses a technique called graphic SPRITES. A *sprite* is a block of graphics memory that can be overlayed onto a graphics screen. One of the nice features of sprites is that they allow a BASIC programmer to simulate depth in a program. Sprites have a priority relating to foreground and background. If a high-priority sprite overlays a low-priority sprite, the low-priority sprite disappears. The advantage of this can be seen when there is only a partial overlay. A tree might be drawn in the foreground using high-priority sprites. An object such as a car stored in a low-priority sprite moving across the screen will disappear as it travels behind the tree. Sprite graphics can be a very powerful animation technique in BASIC.

APPENDIX 4

Maintenance of Microcomputers and Peripherals

The microcomputer has become a fixture in many offices and in quite a few homes, yet preventive maintenance techniques remain a relative mystery. This appendix will help you to make sure that your computer will be around for your use for many years to come. These general-purpose tips are useful for most situations. In all cases, be sure to read your manual and follow all manufacturer's recommendations, as the manufacturer is in the best position to know what the particular machine requires. Do not attempt any of these techniques unless you feel you have a thorough understanding of what is being done. Computers and their accessories are high-technology equipment; refer any servicing to qualified technical personnel. When doing any maintenance, be sure that the device being serviced is off and unplugged.

Fortunately, the computer itself is relatively maintenance-free. The major problems with computers can usually be traced to improper ventilation. Computers typically have cooling slots or holes that should never be restricted. Often, someone will set papers or books on the computer, not realizing that he or she is blocking the vents, which can be a hazardous situation for the computer. Be cautious of mounting computer equipment in high-temperature environments, or of mounting computers in closed cabinets. In either case, be sure to provide a ventilation fan to keep air moving throughout the enclosure.

To check the operation of your computer, locate and purchase a good diagnostic program. A diagnostic program will test all computer functions and report the results. Follow the instructions that come with the software, and it will step you through memory tests, drive or cassette tests, expansion port tests, and any other specific hardware tests required on your system. It is reassuring to run a diagnostic on a regular basis and log the results. Some computers do a simple diagnostic each time they are powered up.

Keyboards require little maintenance, but the keys should be kept clean and covered when not in use to keep dust out of the switch contacts. If keys become sticky or bounce (several letters appear on the screen when you only pressed the key once), the board will require maintenance. In many cases, a professional will remove the keyboard and clean it thoroughly, which will usually restore proper operation.

Disk drives require maintenance on a regular basis. The two major problem areas with disks are dirty read/write heads and drive timing problems. Cleaning drive heads is easy with the number of high-quality drive-cleaning kits on the market. These kits usually consist of a small bottle of cleaning solution and a cleaning pad in a standard disk case.

To clean the heads, moisten the opening on the cleaning diskette with a small amount of solution, and insert the disk into the drive in a normal manner. A 30-second drive access will clean the head, and you can move on to the next drive. Probably the easiest way to cause the drive to activate is to try to access the directory. A DIR or CATALOG command will set the drive in motion, and the drive will search in vain for the directory track. Drive motion will stop after a few seconds with an I/O error message. Continue to access the drive until the motor has run about 30 seconds total.

Disk timing is a little bit more difficult to test and adjust. There are timing programs on the market that will display a disk tachometer on the monitor, reading a relative speed value and a range of acceptability. If the drive speed is out of range, a simple control adjustment can put the drive back into specification. If you are technically oriented, you may wish to make this adjustment yourself.

If you don't have a timing program, you may wish to remove the drive from its case and check the flywheel (a large wheel usually connected to the motor via a drive belt). Often, there are strobe markings on the wheel that can be viewed under a fluorescent light. Adjust the drive speed control until the strobe bars seem to stand still under the fluorescent light. You may need to have a service manual to identify which control is the speed adjust. Do not experiment with a disk drive's internal controls; drive units are expensive and rather delicate high-technology equipment. Errors can be costly.

If your timing program or fluorescent light indicates erratic speed changes, send the drive in for professional service. A problem of this nature cannot usually be corrected by adjustment and indicates a problem in motor speed regulation.

Cassette recorder maintenance is similar, though there are few cassette diagnostics of the caliber of their disk counterparts. A good-quality cassette-cleaning tape will provide all the equipment needed to keep the tape head in good shape. Speed adjustments cannot be made on most recorders, so speed variation problems should be referred to a qualified technician.

Next to disk drives, printers require the most preventive maintenance. Ribbons should be changed whenever the print becomes light, rather than using a heavier strike. This is because many ribbons are lubricated to assist the print head. Older ribbons tend to have less lubricating properties.

Use a small brush or other soft material to remove bits of paper, dust, hair, and so on, from within the printing area. Cleanliness is important around printers. Be careful when working around any gears or levers. Try not to remove any lubricant from parts that require lubrication.

The slide bar that the print head moves on requires occasional lubrication. Follow your owner's manual for specifications on which type of lubricant to use and how often lubrication should be performed.

Monitors require little preventive maintenance but should be well ventilated, and the CRT should be cleaned occasionally with a soft cloth and glass cleaner. If you have a glare screen in front of the CRT, be sure to remove it before cleaning the glass.

If computer operation becomes erratic, unplug all equipment from the AC line. Remove and reinsert any connectors that connect the computer to its peripherals. In many cases, oxidation on connector contacts is responsible for erratic operation, and reinserting connectors is usually enough to remove excess oxidation. Connections may be unplugged and cleaned with a cotton swab moistened with isopropyl alcohol. Let the alcohol evaporate and reinsert the connector.

Edge connectors on circuit cards are often prone to contact oxidation. Remove the cards and clean the conductor contacts with alcohol and a cotton swab. Never remove or reinstall circuit cards in equipment with the power connected. To do so could severely damage your equipment.

Preventive maintenance can be done on a regular basis by anyone if a little care and common sense are applied. To be sure your maintenance won't cause more problems than it cures, follow these simple rules:

1. Always unplug the computer and all of its peripherals before working on them.
2. Always follow the manufacturer's recommendations when performing any procedure.
3. Never continue with a procedure that you are unsure of or do not feel confident that you can do.
4. Refer any servicing of computer-related problems to qualified technical personnel.

By following these tips and techniques, you can be assured that your computer will provide useful and lasting service to you or your business.

APPENDIX 5

Computer Data File Handling

Data storage and retrieval is one of the most useful applications of the microcomputer. By following the techniques described in this appendix, you will be able to have a better understanding of data handling and be more adept at converting data file programs from one computer to another.

Data storage syntax in BASIC varies greatly from one computer to another, yet virtually all computers handle data in similar formats. This appendix will describe and explain the general file-handling techniques.

All computer files can be compared to the standard office file cabinet. Think of the computer storage device (disk or tape drive) as the file cabinet itself. Within the file are records (file folders), each pertaining to one item, whether it be a customer, a part in stock, or any other item that might be stored as part of a file.

Within each record, the information is broken into categories, each category being a subdivision of a record. With a customer file, these categories might be first name, last name, account number, address, city, state, zip code, phone number, balance due, and so on. The correct term for these categories is *field*.

The smallest unit within a field is simply an individual character, and each field is usually composed of a fixed number of characters. For example, the standard state field will contain two characters, which would be the standard postal abbreviation for the desired state. Keep the hierarchy of character, field, record, and file in mind as we discuss files and how they are organized.

The simplest file structure is called a *sequential file* and is often used in any processing where nearly every record must be accessed each time the data are needed. Cassette systems and disk systems generate sequential access files.

We wili use a hypothetical mailing list and detail the steps required to write and read the file. A sequential access mailing list would be used whenever nearly every name is accessed on a periodic basis, such as in a newsletter subscription application.

Though the syntax of each computer varies, virtually all computers use the same process when file handling in BASIC. Typically, the first step is to OPEN the desired file, which can be either a tape or disk file. A single sequential file may only be open for either reading or writing at one time, but not both. The computer must be told whether it is to write or read the file being opened. On some computers, this is done in the open statement, while on others it is done with a separate READ or WRITE statement. The open statement will usually specify which device is being written to or read from (disk, tape, comm link, and so on).

Once the file is opened for writing, the first entry can be placed in the file. Most computers use PRINT or one of its options to put the data in the file. Some computers will allow a WRITE command to put data in a sequential file. If you have WRITE, check your BASIC manual for the advantages of using the WRITE command. A loop can be created that can transfer data from memory into the file.

Once all names are written in the file, use CLOSE to exit the routine. CLOSE is used for two reasons. First, data are placed on the disk or tape in blocks. If the data don't exactly fill a block, they will not be placed on the media. Second, a marker must be written at the end of the file to tell the operating system that there are no more data in the file. CLOSE will write the last block of file information to the media and then write a file marker. If a file is not closed properly, you will receive error messages when you try to retrieve the data. Additionally, some data may be missing.

To open a file for reading, the procedure is similar. The file must be opened in the read mode, and INPUT or one of its options is used to retrieve the data. Before each new input of data from the file, a check for the end-of-file marker must be made. If you try to input data past the end of the file, an error message will appear. After all the data are retrieved, it is necessary to close the file.

With sequential files, virtually all computers follow the above format. Check your BASIC manual for syntax on your computer. If you are doing a program conversion, look up keywords you don't understand in the dictionary to see what that particular command does. Substitute the proper syntax for your computer.

Random access files are similar to but have different capacities than sequential access files. Tape systems are not capable of handling files in random form. If you wish to retrieve a name from a sequential file, the computer must read all data from the beginning of the file until it comes to the desired name.

A random access file has the ability to access any record in the file without reading through the entire file. The file has this capacity because each record is exactly the same number of characters. For example, the hundredth record in a 50-character-per-record file will start at the five-thousandth character. Random access files are used whenever it is likely that not all records will be accessed each time the file is opened. A good example of a random access application is an inventory program. Most of the time, the computer operator wants to check the status of a particular part. It is best to access only the part, rather than have to read through all of the unwanted parts until the computer comes to the desired part. The major constraints regarding random files are that field length must be specified in advance, fields that are too long must be truncated to fit the field space within the record, and short fields must be padded with spaces to fit within the field.

As in sequential access files, random access files must be opened. Next, field quantity and length must be defined. Once the file is opened, records in a random file can be either written to or read from. Records are usually accessed by a record number, and usual syntax to write or read a record is PUT or GET, respectively. A record can be PUT into a file, or you can use GET to retrieve a record. When file access is completed, the file must be closed.

File handling is not complex, but program conversions can be confusing. Before trying any complex program conversions, be sure you understand file-handling techniques on your computer thoroughly. Though the syntax is different on different machines, if you understand how file handling operates on your computer, it is a simple matter to use the dictionary to look up syntax on the program you are converting. Once you see the process, rewrite the routine to fit the syntax of your computer.

Be sure to test and debug any program conversions with all manner of data before putting the program into service. Fill the files with dummy data, and try to catch problems before putting them into important applications. Bugs can appear in unusual places, so be sure to test every element of the program thoroughly.

ASCII Code Chart

Decimal	Character	Hexadecimal	Comments
000	NUL	00	Null
001	SOH	01	Start of Heading
002	STX	02	Start of Text
003	ETX	03	End of Text
004	EOT	04	End of Transmission
005	ENQ	05	Enquiry
006	ACK	06	Acknowledge
007	BEL	07	Bell
008	BS	08	Backspace
009	HT	09	Horizontal Tab
010	LF	0A	Line Feed
011	VT	0B	Vertical Tab
012	FF	0C	Form Feed
013	CR	0D	Carriage Return
014	SO	0E	Shift Out
015	SI	0F	Shift In
016	DLE	10	Data Link Escape
017	DC1	11	Device Control 1
018	DC2	12	Device Control 2
019	DC3	13	Device Control 3
020	DC4	14	Device Control 4
021	NAK	15	Not Acknowledged
022	SYN	16	Synchronous Idle
023	ETB	17	End of Transmission Block

Decimal	Character	Hexadecimal	Comments
024	CAN	18	Cancel
025	EM	19	End of Medium
026	SUB	1A	Substitute
027	ESC	1B	Escape
028	FS	1C	File Separator
029	GS	1D	Group Separator
030	RS	1E	Record Separator
031	US	1F	Unit Separator
032	SP	20	Space
033	!	21	
034	"	22	
035	#	23	
036	$	24	
037	%	25	
038	&	26	
039	'	27	
040	(	28	
041	)	29	
042	*	2A	
043	+	2B	
044	,	2C	
045	-	2D	
046	.	2E	
047	/	2F	
048	0	30	
049	1	31	
050	2	32	
051	3	33	
052	4	34	
053	5	35	
054	6	36	
055	7	37	
056	8	38	
057	9	39	
058	:	3A	
059	;	3B	
060	<	3C	
061	=	3D	
062	>	3E	
063	?	3F	

Decimal	Character	Hexadecimal	Comments
064	@	40	
065	A	41	
066	B	42	
067	C	43	
068	D	44	
069	E	45	
070	F	46	
071	G	47	
072	H	48	
073	I	49	
074	J	4A	
075	K	4B	
076	L	4C	
077	M	4D	
078	N	4E	
079	O	4F	
080	P	50	
081	Q	51	
082	R	52	
083	S	53	
084	T	54	
085	U	55	
086	V	56	
087	W	57	
088	X	58	
089	Y	59	
090	Z	5A	
091	[	5B	
092	\	5C	
093	]	5D	
094	↑	5E	Up Arrow
095	—	5F	Underscore
096	`	60	Accent
097	a	61	
098	b	62	
099	c	63	
100	d	64	
101	e	65	
102	f	66	
103	g	67	

Decimal	Character	Hexadecimal	Comments
104	h	68	
105	i	69	
106	j	6A	
107	k	6B	
108	l	6C	
109	m	6D	
110	n	6E	
111	o	6F	
112	p	70	
113	q	71	
114	r	72	
115	s	73	
116	t	74	
117	u	75	
118	v	76	
119	w	77	
120	x	78	
121	y	79	
122	z	7A	
123	{	7B	Left Curly Brace
124	|	7C	Vertical Bar
125	}	7D	Right Curly Brace
126	~	7E	Tilde
127	DEL	7F	Delete

APPENDIX 7

Base Conversion Chart

Decimal	Octal	Hexadecimal
000	000	00
001	001	01
002	002	02
003	003	03
004	004	04
005	005	05
006	006	06
007	007	07
008	010	08
009	011	09
010	012	0A
011	013	0B
012	014	0C
013	015	0D
014	016	0E
015	017	0F
016	020	10
017	021	11
018	022	12
019	023	13
020	024	14
021	025	15
022	026	16
023	027	17

Decimal	Octal	Hexadecimal
024	030	18
025	031	19
026	032	1A
027	033	1B
028	034	1C
029	035	1D
030	036	1E
031	037	1F
032	040	20
033	041	21
034	042	22
035	043	23
036	044	24
037	045	25
038	046	26
039	047	27
040	050	28
041	051	29
042	052	2A
043	053	2B
044	054	2C
045	055	2D
046	056	2E
047	057	2F
048	060	30
049	061	31
050	062	32
051	063	33
052	064	34
053	065	35
054	066	36
055	067	37
056	070	38
057	071	39
058	072	3A
059	073	3B
060	074	3C
061	075	3D
062	076	3E
063	077	3F

Decimal	Octal	Hexadecimal
064	100	40
065	101	41
066	102	42
067	103	43
068	104	44
069	105	45
070	106	46
071	107	47
072	110	48
073	111	49
074	112	4A
075	113	4B
076	114	4C
077	115	4D
078	116	4E
079	117	4F
080	120	50
081	121	51
082	122	52
083	123	53
084	124	54
085	125	55
086	126	56
087	127	57
088	130	58
089	131	59
090	132	5A
091	133	5B
092	134	5C
093	135	5D
094	136	5E
095	137	5F
096	140	60
097	141	61
098	142	62
099	143	63
100	144	64
101	145	65
102	146	66
103	147	67

Decimal	Octal	Hexadecimal
104	150	68
105	151	69
106	152	6A
107	153	6B
108	154	6C
109	155	6D
110	156	6E
111	157	6F
112	160	70
113	161	71
114	162	72
115	163	73
116	164	74
117	165	75
118	166	76
119	167	77
120	170	78
121	171	79
122	172	7A
123	173	7B
124	074	7C
125	175	7D
126	176	7E
127	177	7F

Commonly Found Error Types

ERROR TYPE	COMMENTS
ALREADY EXISTS	You tried to rename a file to an existing name.
ALREADY OPEN	You tried to open a file that was already open.
BAD RECORD NUMBER	Random access record number too high or low.
CAN'T CONTINUE	You tried to continue a program after an END statement or error.
DIRECT STATEMENT IN FILE	Program being read in from disk or tape has a line with no line number.
DISK FULL	There is no more room on the disk.
DIVIDE BY ZERO	A division occurred when the divisor variable was zero.
FIELD TOO LONG	The sum of field lengths is larger than the record length.
FILE MODE	You tried to load a BINARY file using BASIC program syntax or vice versa.
FILE NOT FOUND	The disk does not contain the file you specified.

ERROR TYPE	COMMENTS
ILLEGAL DIRECT COMMAND	You issued a command that can only be issued in program mode.
ILLEGAL FILENAME	The filename you specified is in incorrect format.
ILLEGAL FUNCTION CALL	You tried to call a BASIC function with an improper argument.
INPUT/OUTPUT	The computer is having trouble reading or writing to the disk or tape.
INPUT PAST END OF RECORD	You specified a record number greater than the last record in the file.
LONG STRING	The string is too long to be handled by BASIC.
MISSING OPERAND	The computer does not have enough data to finish the operation.
NEXT WITHOUT FOR	The program encountered a NEXT statement before being issued a FOR.
OUT OF DATA	There are more READ statements than DATA amounts in your program.
OUT OF MEMORY	You have exceeded the memory requirements of your computer.
OUT OF STRING SPACE	There is not enough string storage space for the number of strings you have defined.
OVERFLOW	Numbers were so large that they exceeded the capacity of the interpreter.
REDIMENSIONED ARRAY	You have tried to dimension an array more than once in the same program.
RESUME WITHOUT ERROR	The program encountered a RESUME statement before an error occurred.

ERROR TYPE	COMMENTS
RETURN WITHOUT GOSUB	The program encountered a RETURN statement before being issued a GOSUB.
SUBSCRIPT OUT OF RANGE	You used an array number larger than what the array was dimensioned to.
SYNTAX	The command is not in the computer vocabulary.
TOO MANY FILES	Too many files have been opened at one time.
TYPE MISMATCH	You tried to assign a string to a numeric variable or vice versa.
UNDEFINED LINE	You used GOTO or GOSUB to call a nonexistent line.
UNDEFINED USER FUNCTION	A user function was called before it was defined.

APPENDIX 9

Derived Functions

Some functions that cannot be performed directly in BASIC may be performed by using these derived functions.

FUNCTION	BASIC EQUIVALENT
SECANT	SEC (X) = 1/COS (X)
COSECANT	CSC (X) = 1/SIN (X)
COTANGENT	COT (X) = 1/TAN (X)
INVERSE SINE	ARCSIN (X) = ATN (X/SQR (− X*X + 1))
INVERSE COSINE	ARCCOS (X) = − ATN (X/SQR (− X*X + 1)) + PI/2
INVERSE SECANT	ARCSEC (X) = ATN (X/SQR (X*X − 1))
INVERSE COSECANT	ARCCSC (X) = ATN (X/SQR (X*X − 1)) + (SGN (X) − 1*PI/2)
INVERSE COTANGENT	ARCOT (X) = ATN (X) + PI/2
HYPERBOLIC SINE	SINH (X) = (EXP (X) − EXP (− X))/2
HYPERBOLIC COSINE	COSH (X) = (EXP (X) + EXP (− X))/2

FUNCTION	BASIC EQUIVALENT
HYPERBOLIC TANGENT	TANH (X) = EXP (− X)/(EXP (X) + EXP (− X)) *2 + 1
HYPERBOLIC SECANT	SECH (X) = 2/(EXP (X) + EXP (− X))
HYPERBOLIC COSECANT	CSCH (X) = 2/EXP (X) − EXP (− X))
HYPERBOLIC COTANGENT	COTH (X) = EXP (− X)/(EXP (X) − EXP (− X)) *2 + 1
INVERSE HYPERBOLIC SINE	ARCSINH (X) = LOG (X + SQR (X*X + 1))
INVERSE HYPERBOLIC COSINE	ARCCOSH (X) = LOG (X + SQR (X*X − 1))
INVERSE HYPERBOLIC TANGENT	ARCTANH (X) = LOG ((1 + X)/(1 − X))/2
INVERSE HYPERBOLIC SECANT	ARCSECH (X) = LOG ((SQR (− X*X + 1) + 1/X)
INVERSE HYPERBOLIC COSECANT	ARCCSCH (X) = LOG ((SGN (X) *SQR (X*X + 1/X)
INVERSE HYPERBOLIC COTANGENT	ARCCOTH (X) = LOG ((X + 1)/(X − 1))/2

APPENDIX 10

Bibliography of BASIC Source Materials

The following list of books represents an excellent source of information regarding the individual computers discussed. In some cases, these were the references used in creating *The Standard BASIC Dictionary for Programming.*

Albrect, Inman, and Zamora. *Introduction to TI BASIC.* Rochelle Park, N.J.: Hayden Book Company, 1980.

Carris. *Inside Atari BASIC.* Reston, Va.: Reston Publishing Company, 1983.

Commodore. *Commodore 64 User's Guide.* Indianapolis: Commodore Business Machines, Inc., and Howard W. Sams and Company, 1982.

Conrad, Goldstein, and Zimmerman. *Osborne User's Guide Applications and Programming.* Bowie, Md.: Robert J. Brady Company, 1983.

Haskell. *Apple BASIC.* Englewood Cliffs, N.J.: Prentice-Hall, Inc., 1982.

Haskell. *TRS–80 Extended Color BASIC.* Englewood Cliffs, N.J.: Prentice-Hall, Inc., 1983.

Held. *IBM PC BASIC.* New York: John Wiley and Sons, Inc., 1982.

Hergert. *The Timex/Sinclair 1000 BASIC Handbook.* Berkeley: Sybex, Inc., 1983.

Lewis. *Using the Osborne 1 Computer.* Reston, Va.: Reston Publishing Company, 1983.

Parker. *TRS–80 Disk BASIC for Business.* Reston, Va.: Reston Publishing Company, 1980, 1981, 1982.

Spencer. *Programming the TRS–80 Pocket Computer.* Englewood Cliffs, N.J.: Prentice-Hall, Inc., 1982.

References to Applesoft BASIC from Apple Computer, Inc., 20525 Mariani, Cupertino, CA 95014, 1982.

References to Color Computer Disk System BASIC from the Color Computer Disk System Manual. Tandy Corporation, 1981.

References to Tandy Radio Shack Disk BASIC from the Disk System Owner's Manual. Tandy Corporation, 1980.

References to Tandy Radio Shack BASIC from the Operation and BASIC Language Reference Manual. Tandy Corporation, 1980.

FOR REFERENCE
not to be taken from this room

Norma E. Hagan Library
Cumberland College
Williamsburg, Ky. 40769